A Short Book about Paul

A Short Book about Paul

The Servant of Jesus

Paul Barnett

CASCADE *Books* • Eugene, Oregon

A SHORT BOOK ABOUT PAUL
The Servant of Jesus

Copyright © 2019 Paul Barnett. All rights reserved. Except for brief quotations in critical publications or reviews, no part of this book may be reproduced in any manner without prior written permission from the publisher. Write: Permissions, Wipf and Stock Publishers, 199 W. 8th Ave., Suite 3, Eugene, OR 97401.

Cascade Books
An Imprint of Wipf and Stock Publishers
199 W. 8th Ave., Suite 3
Eugene, OR 97401

www.wipfandstock.com

PAPERBACK ISBN: 978-1-5326-6554-7
HARDCOVER ISBN: 978-1-5326-6555-4
EBOOK ISBN: 978-1-5326-6556-1

Cataloguing-in-Publication data:

Names: Barnett, Paul, author.

Title: A short book about Paul : the servant of Jesus / by Paul Barnett.

Description: Eugene, OR: Cascade Books, 2019 | Series: if applicable | Includes bibliographical references and index.

Identifiers: ISBN 978-1-5326-6554-7 (paperback) | ISBN 978-1-5326-6555-4 (hardcover) | ISBN 978-1-5326-6556-1 (ebook)

Subjects: LCSH: Paul, the Apostle, Saint. | Bible. Epistles of Paul—Theology.

Classification: BS2505 B15 2019 (print) | BS2505 (ebook)

Manufactured in the U.S.A.   JULY 11, 2019

In memory of Donald William Bradley Robinson
Teacher

T. R. Glover, mindful that Nero Caesar condemned Paul,
declared that the day would come
when people would call their dog Nero and their sons PAUL.

Table of Contents

Preface ix

1. The Greatness of Paul 1
2. Dating Paul 9
3. Paul's Story 1: The First Thirty Years (AD 4–34) 16
4. Paul's Story 2: His Second Thirty Years (AD 34–65) 31
5. Paul's Message: God's Son 50
6. The Example and Teaching of Jesus 57
7. Paul's Vision: The Unification of Humanity 66
8. Paul's "Traditions" 70
9. Paul's Mission Network 78
10. Paul's Mission Coworkers 83
11. The Importance of Membership 110
12. Paul's Spiritual World 116
13. Paul and the Christian Mind 120
14. Paul's Concerns 126
15. Problems with Paul 135
16. Three Questions about Paul 147
17. A New Perspective on Paul? 153
18. The Legacy of Paul 159

Bibliography 173

Name and Subject Index 175

Scripture Index 179

Preface

PAUL IS A CONTROVERSIAL and divisive figure. Some hail him as the God-given interpreter and apologist for Jesus. For many within modern Western culture, however, his influence is regarded as having been deeply unhelpful.

His considerable missionary achievements and the survival of his letters in our Bibles means that for many, Paul is placed alongside Jesus as having had a superior and unwarranted influence.

Jesus was the doer of acts of kindness and a teacher of profound values, whereas Paul introduced guilt-ridden doctrines of original sin and blood-based redemption. Furthermore, he articulated harsh teachings about homosexuality and male-to-female domination, matters about which Jesus said nothing.

Jesus was a teacher and exemplar of love, but Paul was the teacher and exemplar of judgmental and unkind doctrines. At a personal level, he is seen as aloof and uncaring. In the minds of many, therefore, Jesus is thought of positively but Paul is thought of negatively.

However, when we investigate Paul in more detail we discover that the noun "love" and the verb "to love" (that is, "love" understood sacrificially), occur with remarkable frequency in his writings and far exceed appearances in the Gospels or the other literature in the New Testament. Paul repeatedly sums his message up as "faith," "hope," and "love," but "love" is the greatest.

As well, when we consider references to prayer in the New Testament we find a remarkable concentration of teaching about thanksgiving and intercession in Paul's writings. The same applies to "joy" and "rejoice."

To those who knew him it is evidence that Paul the apostle was much loved and revered by the members of his churches. He was deeply affected by problems in the churches as they arose, especially among the Corinthian believers.

It is hoped that the following "short" book about Paul will be informative and go some distance in helping readers better understand this interesting man.

This brief study of Paul is conscious that most books about him are anything but "short." Of the many longer books on Paul let me mention three that are worthy of serious study. The first is Jerome Murphy-O'Connor, *Paul: A Critical Life* (Oxford University Press, 1997), which usefully supplies many details about Paul's social context. Another is Tom Wright, *Paul: A Biography* (SPCK, 2018), where the author locates the apostle within the Bible's overarching story. For me, however, I feel a special debt of gratitude for F. F. Bruce, *Paul: Apostle of the Free Spirit* (Paternoster, 1977), whose matter of fact, common sense approach I have found especially endearing.

I once heard an eminent scholar of antiquity remark that he was a follower of Jesus and an admirer of Paul. That is an attitude that I have come to hold. Paul was not a perfect person, but he left an astonishing legacy, which I hope will emerge from this not very long book.

One

The Greatness of Paul

JESUS WAS A PUBLIC figure for only four years, between AD 29–33. During those years he gathered twelve disciples, taught in public and private, cast out demons and healed the sick, debated with other rabbis, and was crucified in Jerusalem where he was resurrected from the dead. In just over twenty years (from AD 34–57) Paul had established Christianity in a vast arc from Arabia around to and including Macedonia that was effectively a quarter of the land space of the Roman Empire. In the following centuries the lands in which Paul established churches became the world center of Christianity, based in Constantinople, capital of the Eastern Roman Empire.

By AD 64, as the great historian Tacitus noted, the Christians in Rome had become a "vast multitude," a suitably large scapegoat to blame for the fire that destroyed most of the world capital in that year.

There were many of Jesus' early followers who spread the message about him during those decades, but the greatest of them was a man named Paul. In fact, it is difficult to think of the astonishing growth of early Christianity apart from him. James Dunn claimed that "it was Paul more than any other single person who ensured that the new movement stemming from Jesus would become a truly international and truly intellectually coherent religion."[1]

Equally remarkable was Paul's role in changing the Jesus movement from being narrowly and exclusively Jewish to being open to non-Jews as well. Paul deliberately travelled through gentile lands to invite their people to embrace the Jewish Messiah, Jesus. Dramatically, he insisted that the

1. Dunn, *Theology of Paul the Apostle*, 2–3.

followers of Jesus did not first have to become Jewish proselytes. Faith in Jesus, expressed in baptism, was sufficient and was not to be compromised by demands for male circumcision, adherence to Jewish food and purity laws, or obedience to the religious calendar.

In the many churches that Paul established, the majority of the members were gentiles. Before his conversion, Paul had been a leading younger Pharisee, as he said, "a Hebrew of Hebrews." There is nothing more astonishing about Paul than his outreach to the non-Jews, all the more so since he himself steadfastly remained a Jew to the end of his life.

Paul's unique achievements—effectively founding Christianity as a world movement and without the requirement of converts adopting Jewish practices—are quite noteworthy when we consider his circumstances. Paul faced ferocious opposition from gentile culture that was based on the gods of Greece and Rome, but no less was he opposed by those Jewish Christians who insisted that gentile converts must adopt Jewish practices.

Paul the missionary had no money but had to work during the night as a tent maker to support himself and his companions. He had no political influence, but was publicly flogged on many occasions. He travelled vast distances, mostly by foot, through forbidding mountains and harsh countryside. He was often alone, without companions, as he was in Arabia and Athens.

Martin Hengel wrote appreciatively that Paul's mission was "unique in the ancient world" and "an unprecedented happening in terms both of the history of religion in antiquity and of later church history" and that as a result of what he did Paul "has remained unparalleled over the subsequent 1900 years."[2]

Several things help explain Paul's achievements, the most important of which was the depth of his personal devotion to the crucified but resurrected Jesus. On the road to Damascus the heavenly Jesus confronted Paul, the would-be destroyer of the new "faith." Immediately after being baptized he began preaching the faith he had attempted to destroy. Thirty years later, knowing that his own death was near, he wrote passionately about longing to meet with the one whom he had unswervingly served throughout those years.[3] For the thirty years from his conversion near Damascus to his death in Rome it was his love for Jesus that inspired Paul and drove him on.

---

2. Hengel, *Between Jesus and Paul*, 49–50.
3. Phil 3:10.

This is the more remarkable since Paul had not, so far as we know, ever met the man Jesus. As well, the Jesus whom Paul served came from a lower social and educational stratum. Jesus was a self-educated man who followed the trade of his stepfather Joseph, a builder. By contrast, Paul was a privileged citizen of his home city, Tarsus, and by birth a Roman citizen. From his teen years Paul had been educated in Jerusalem under Gamaliel, the greatest rabbi of his day.

How do we explain Paul's passionate devotion to one who, humanly speaking, was his social and economic inferior? It was because the Jesus who addressed him did so from the brightness of heaven, convincing Paul that Jesus was actually the eternal Son of God who had given his life for Paul the persecutor to have a right standing with God and be blessed with the presence and power of the Spirit of God. Paul spoke movingly of "the Son of God who loved me and gave himself for me."[4] God directed Paul to proclaim the Son of God "among the gentiles," law-free and grace-based.[5]

It was Paul's sense of Christ's love for him that drove him and inspired him to the very end of his life. As he said in just a few words, "the love of Christ controls us."[6] His pronoun "us" includes his fellow believers but we are in no doubt that Paul was speaking primarily about his sense of Christ's love for *him*.

The measure of Paul's devoted service of Jesus was the degree to which he suffered for him. In Damascus at the time of his baptism, Paul was told "how much he must suffer" for the sake of Jesus' name.[7] He was flogged five times with the thirty-nine lashes in Jewish synagogues, beaten with rods three times by Roman sergeants, endured numerous imprisonments, countless beatings, once being stoned, twice being shipwrecked, and was often near death.[8] He spent almost ten of his thirty years as a Christian in prison. He writes of "sharing abundantly in Christ's sufferings."[9] He knew first-hand the reality he spoke about to the Christians in Philippi: "It has been granted to you that for the sake of Christ you should not only believe in him but also *suffer* for his sake."[10]

4. Gal 2:20.
5. Gal 1:16.
6. 2 Cor 5:14.
7. Acts 9:16.
8. 2 Cor 11:23–25.
9. 2 Cor 1:5.
10. Phil 1:29.

If we are looking for the great motive that drove Paul, from which he never deviated, we will find it in just one thing: his sense of being loved by Christ, which he embraced in return by his love for Jesus expressed in the hard work of serving him.

Important elements explaining his achievements were his intellect and education, his strategic leadership and his remarkable skills in letter writing. Critical as these were, however, it was his sense of being loved by the Lord, which he reciprocated, that explains the achievements of Paul the apostle.

Paul's letters reveal him to have been endowed with a sharp but subtle intellect. Anthony Flew, a leading atheist philosopher of the twentieth century, who later changed his mind and adopted theism, said that Paul was "a first class intellectual" who had "a brilliant philosophical mind."[11] That is high praise from one of the great philosophical leaders in modern times.

His remarkable intellect was shaped by a privileged education. Paul's early years in Tarsus would have exposed him to the text of the Bible, both in the home and in the synagogue. Later, from the time of his youth in Jerusalem under Rabbi Gamaliel, Paul was subject to rigorous instruction in the Bible, but also in the traditions of the rabbis.

His letters and speeches recorded in the book of Acts reveal a man steeped in the Greek version of the Bible, the so-called Septuagint. Those letters and speeches tell us that Paul the Christian scoured the Old Testament to locate texts that promised the expected Messiah. His letters frequently quote Old Testament texts that Paul adapted in terms of their fulfillment in Christ.

Paul was a brilliant strategist. He typically went to cities that satisfied key criteria: port cities and crossroads cities with their many passing travellers; cities with synagogues where he would seek converts who were biblically literate; and cities that were Roman colonies where his Roman citizenship would protect him. These were among the key criteria that directed Paul's choice of locations for ministry. From these nodal points the message of Jesus would spread far and wide.

Paul's usual pattern was to take the message of Jesus the Christ first to the synagogues. In Ephesus he taught daily for three years in a hired lecture hall. Paul gathered new believers into house-based meetings, which was a prudent procedure because the Romans outlawed unofficial assemblies. Typically these house-churches had between 50 and 100 members. The

---

11. Flew, *There Is a God*, 157, 185–86.

"*whole* church" in Corinth met in the home of Gaius, suggesting there were also smaller, house-based meetings.¹²

Paul was an inspiring leader who gradually created a network of colleagues he called "fellow-workers" and "fellow-soldiers" who assisted him in the churches and who travelled on his behalf to distant churches to supervise and encourage. We know the names of forty of these associates. Paul called the members of the church by familial names, "brother" and "sister" who greeted one another with a holy kiss when they met.

Paul directed his churches to model their attitudes and behavior according to the example of Jesus, for example, his humility, his meekness and gentleness, his search for the lost, and his welcome of those who came to him.¹³

Paul himself looked to the example of Jesus in these matters, but also encouraged the churches to follow his own example. Paul worked to provide for himself. He depended on Christ, not "works of the law," to be "right" with God. He prized humility not arrogance in sensitively seeking the good of his neighbor.¹⁴ Paul is easily misunderstood as presenting himself as a perfect man but on the contrary, he said he was the "chief" of sinners.¹⁵ Rather, he identified key aspects of Jesus' character and carefully lived these out as a father giving living examples for his spiritual children to follow.

We know Paul today through a new form of letter that he pioneered. Churches throughout the world continue to read his letters in their public meetings. Small groups appreciatively analyze and pray over passages from the letters of Paul. Individual Christians read and prayerfully reflect on his words.

Paul does not write conventional letters like those between friends and family. Rather his letters were longer, to be read aloud to the gathered churches, and also to be read repeatedly as "scripture" and copied and shared with other churches.

He employed a wide variety of styles, including thanksgiving prayers, personal memoirs, ironic speeches, collections of Old Testament texts, allegories, apocalyptic and wisdom motifs, sublimely lyrical hymns, creeds,

---

12. Rom 16:23; 1 Cor 14:23.

13. Christ's humility (Phil 2:5; 2 Cor 8:9); Christ's meekness (2 Cor 10:1); Christ's search for and welcoming of the lost (1 Cor 10:33—11:1; Rom 15:7).

14. As a worker (2 Thess 3:7, 9); in faith (Phil 3:17); in humility (1 Cor 4:16); in love of neighbor (1 Cor 11:1).

15. 1 Tim 1:15.

formulaic teaching passages, and blazingly confronting admonitions. This wide variety within his letters makes them always fresh and interesting. As a letter writer Paul adapted existing letter formats in such a way that he established a new literary genre.[16]

In sum, the motive for Paul's unique, world-changing achievement was the "love of Jesus," which he exercised through a powerful, well-educated intellect, innovative strategy, inspirational leadership and example, and brilliant letter-writing skills.

Accordingly, the Jewish man Paul, the apostle of Jesus, remains the most influential person from the classical era. Great Greek and Roman philosophers, writers, engineers, architects, politicians, and soldiers have left their imprint on history but no one has come close to Paul in terms of his ongoing influence. Jesus was the founder of what has become the world's greatest religion, but its initial propagation and explanation owes an unrivalled debt to Paul.

Scholars and laypeople analyze and pore over his words. Encyclopedic commentaries on his letters continue to be published. His missionary methods and exploits continue to inspire missionaries and pastors. His interpretation of Jesus' theology and love-based ethic continues to inform the minds and direct the wills of millions of people.

Paul's Critics

However, Paul had his critics back then—the Corinthian Christians and James, brother of Jesus, for example—as he continues to have his detractors today.[17]

In the early centuries Jewish Christian groups like the Ebionites voiced implied criticisms of Paul. They required circumcision, Sabbath observance, and adherence of Levitical dietary rules. The Ebionites denied that "faith alone" was sufficient for salvation and rejected Paul's authority, regarding him as an apostate from the Law of Moses. Their name, "Ebionite," means "poor" and some have suggested that they were the successors of the poor saints in Jerusalem for whom Paul organized the collection of money from the gentile churches. Alternatively, however, mainstream gentile Christians may have thought of their theology as "poverty stricken."

---

16. Bird, "Reassessing a Rhetorical Approach," 374–79.

17. For a comprehensive review of Paul's critics see Gray, *Paul as a Problem*. The various quotations following are acknowledged as derived from Gray, *Paul as a Problem*.

While criticism of Paul was rare from within the ancient "catholic" church, the same was not true of Jewish attitudes. The *Nishmat Kol Hay* was a liturgical document from that era for use in the synagogue that may have been a polemic against Paul. Jewish anti-Pauline sentiment continued into the medieval period, in fact right through to today. Paul's negative attitude to the Law branded him as a pseudo-Jew, not a true son of Abraham.

Pagan writers from the early centuries were hostile toward Paul. Porphyry castigated Paul as a liar and hypocrite who gouged money from rich women; Julian the Apostate labelled him "a charlatan."

Although the Qur'an makes no reference to Paul, later Islamic writings castigate him for inventing the notion of Jesus' divinity, violating their creed, "There is no God but Allah." For medieval Muslims, Paul was "a wicked and evil Jew," a hypocrite and a deceiver, who undermined Jewish law and Jewish monotheism.

It was from the era of the Enlightenment, however, that most blows against Paul were struck. G. E. Lessing thought Paul's writings "unintelligible," whereas Christ's teachings were "plain and intelligible." Peter Annet dismissed Paul as a liar and imposter, "the author of a new religion." David Hume wrote that Paul was guilty of "contempt for the common rules of reason." The views of deists Thomas Paine, Thomas Jefferson, Jeremy Bentham, and Richard Carlisle are caustic in the extreme.

Throughout the Enlightenment and later it became fashionable to contrast the bad Paul with the good Jesus. Ernst Renan, for example, wrote, "True Christianity . . . comes from the Gospels—not from the letters of Paul. The writings of Paul have been a hidden rock—the causes of the principle defects of Christian theology."

Friedrich Nietzsche was hostile to both Jesus and Paul, yet he reserved these harsh words for Paul: "the genius in hatred; in the vision of hatred; and the inexorable logic of hatred."

More recently Albert Schweitzer declared: "Greek, Catholic and Protestant theologies all contain the Gospel of Paul in a form that does not continue the Gospel of Jesus, but displaces it." William Wrede famously wrote, "The second founder of Christianity [Paul] has even, compared with the first, exercised the stronger—not the better—influence."

So the list of harsh critics of Paul continues until today, and includes H. L. Mencken, H. G. Wells, George Bernard Shaw, and even Adolph Hitler.

Paul's chief sin was that he eclipsed and replaced Jesus, which is well captured by the Jewish quip, "Jesus was a good boy, but Paul was a bad *goy!*" He was guilty of introducing into theology the notions of divinity, trinity, and redemption, ideas that were foreign to Jesus of Nazareth. Furthermore, he promoted these deviant doctrines in longwinded and opaque arguments.

There was one other fault found in Paul, his inflexible and puritanical view of sex, including his ban on homosexual practice. Many eminent writers, including Ernest Hemingway, Lawrence Durrell, and Gore Vidal have parodied Paul's attitudes toward sex.

In Defense of Paul

Once the apostolic era finished there was no access to Paul the man; he could be accessed only through his writings. Many of his critics, ancient and modern, tend to doubt the reality of his Damascus conversion and display a lack of sympathetic understanding of the complex range of pastoral issues he addressed in his letters. In other words, in the main, his critics do not empathize with Paul the man, his values, or the challenges he faced. They tend not to understand Paul on his terms, but only on theirs.

His views on sexuality, for example, spring from the whole biblical tradition, beginning with the Law of Moses and culminating with the teaching of Jesus. In his ministry to non-Jews at that time, Paul faced values and practices inimical to stable marriage and family life, for example, frequent divorce, adultery, bestiality, sodomy, and the exposure of unwanted children. Before launching into a tirade against Paul's supposed sexual narrowness, potential critics should at least do Paul the favor of understanding the pastoral basis for his views.

The oft-repeated complaint that Paul's redemptive theology deviated from Jesus' homely agrarian aphorisms fails at several points. One is that Jesus' "kingdom" teaching was profoundly redemptive, and the other is that "redemptive" traditions Paul quotes in 1 Corinthians must have been formulated in the Jerusalem church in the immediate aftermath of Jesus. Paul did not invent the words, "Christ died for our sins." These were formulated in Jerusalem under the leadership of Peter who was Jesus' leading disciple.

In a later chapter we will address other problems with Paul.

Two

Dating Paul

Paul's Dates

PAUL'S BIRTH DATE IS difficult to establish. His letters yield no clues so that we are entirely dependent on the Acts of the Apostles. In AD 34[1] the High Priest in Jerusalem at Paul's request provided this "young man"[2] with letters to the Damascus synagogues authorizing him extradite disciples from Damascus.[3] According to Jewish tradition, a man was given "authority" at age thirty[4] so that we assume Paul to have been thirty or older in AD 34 when he set out for Damascus. By this calculation Paul was born ca. AD 4.

Dating Paul's death is not much easier. It appears that he died sometime between the Great Fire of Rome in July AD 64 (after which Nero Caesar scapegoated "vast numbers"[5] of Christians—in AD 65?) and the assassination of the emperor in AD 68. As a Roman citizen, Paul would not have been crucified but most likely beheaded. Paul's Roman citizenship may have preserved his life beyond the mass killing of his fellow-Christians.

---

1. According to Luke 3:1–2 John the Baptist began preaching in Tiberius's fifteenth year as Caesar, that is, in AD 28. If we allow for a period to elapse before Jesus was baptized and for three or more years for his attendance at annual feasts, we arrive at AD 33 as the date of the first Easter, and for Paul's persecutions to have begun about a year later, in AD 34.

2. Acts 7:58.

3. Acts 9:1–3.

4. Mishnah *Aboth* 5.21.

5. Tacitus, *Annals of Imperial Rome* xv.44. The Romans did not crucify Roman citizens.

AD		
4	birth	Tarsus
34	conversion	Damascus
65 [?]	death	Rome

Paul's conversion occurred at his life's mid-point. The dominant influence for his first thirty years was his passion for the Law of Moses. Following his conversion, his passion for Jesus became his new obsession throughout his remaining years.

It is of critical importance to understand Paul's change of heart and the absolute difference this made to him. Otherwise our survey in the following two chapters will be just "one thing after another" and Paul's new life as a servant of Jesus was anything but that.

Knowing about Paul

How do we know about Paul? Historians are dependent on sources, so what are the sources of information for Paul?

Essentially there are two—Paul's own letters and Luke's Acts of the Apostles. There is also *The Acts of Paul and Thecla*, an apocryphal work from the second century, but it is of little value in casting light on the life and achievements of Paul.

Paul's Letters

Evidence from the second century points to a *collection* of Paul's letters. Let me start from ca. AD 200 by referring to three codices, early formatted "books" written on papyrus, which between them contain almost the entire New Testament. These were discovered in the early 1930s in the humidity-free sands of Oxyrhynchus, Middle Egypt.

- P45   The four Gospels and the Acts of the Apostles
- P46   The Letters of Paul and the Letter to the Hebrews
- P47   The Revelation

It is widely accepted that these codices had been assembled for reading in the churches. The codex (book format) was more manageable than cumbersome and heavy scrolls.

Dating Paul

These codices written on papyrus have not escaped the ravages of time unscathed. Some of the sheets are missing, others damaged. Our concern is with P46, which attempts to preserve the entire corpus of Paul's writings (together with the Letter to the Hebrews).[6]

Moving backward we come next to the so-called Muratorian Canon, a body of text dated to ca. AD 180. The canon lists the thirteen letters of Paul, implying the existence of a collection of these texts. As we continue our backward journey we encounter further references to a collection of Paul's corpus—by Polycarp, by the Letter to Diognetus, and by the schismatic Marcion.[7]

Clement of Rome, writing ca. AD 96, cites or echoes Romans, 1 and 2 Corinthians, Galatians, Ephesians, and Philippians, suggesting the existence of a collection of Paul's letters. From the mid-60s we have the second letter of Peter referring to "all his [Paul's] letters,"[8] which could refer to a collection of those letters.

This brief survey leaves little doubt that there was, almost from the time of Paul, a collection of his letters. But who was responsible for that collection? There are two schools of thought. According to some authorities, Paul's letters were progressively collected and retained in the churches throughout the span of Paul's letter writing, from ca. AD 48 to ca. AD 65. We know that Paul requested the copying and exchange of his letters (Col 4:16—"And when this letter has been read among you, have it read in the church of the Laodiceans; and see that you also read the letter from Laodicea.")

Other scholars argue that an individual had gathered the apostle's writing into a single corpus. But who might that have been? Some point to a close associate like Timothy or Luke visiting the churches that had received letters from Paul, copying them and collecting them. Another and more likely suggestion is that Paul and his associates copied the letters at the time of writing.[9] That would explain the apparent dependence in Romans from material in Galatians and 1 Corinthians.

---

6. P46 ends with 1 Thessalonians and has no 2 Thessalonians or Paul's three Pastoral epistles.

7. Marcion's writings have not survived but are only known through his critics, e.g., Tertullian (*Against Marcion* 5). See Porter, "Paul and the Pauline Letter Collection," 19–36.

8. 2 Pet 3:16.

9. See Richards, *Paul and First Century Letter-Writing*, 218–33.

The single collection thesis is the most likely and Paul appears to have been the collector.

Luke

The Acts of the Apostles 13–28 is Luke's account of Paul's travels AD 48–62 from Syrian Antioch to Rome. Most of Paul's letter writing to the churches occurred during those fifteen years.[10] The narrative of Acts makes it possible to locate the places and the dates from which Paul wrote to the churches.

	Written to:	Written from:
48	Galatians	Antioch
50	1 and 2 Thessalonians	Corinth
54	Philemon	
	Colossians	Ephesus
	Ephesians	
55	1 Corinthians	Ephesus
56	2 Corinthians	Berea (?)
57	Romans	Corinth
62	Philippians	Rome

The dates are accurate to within a year or so. If we only possessed the letters and did not have the Acts of the Apostles, or had no confidence in that text, we could not chart Paul's movements during those years nor locate times and places of letter-writing.

So the question is: what confidence can we have that Luke's Acts is a reliable source for Paul's travels and activities?

When evaluating information about Paul it has become customary to assign priority to his letters over the book of Acts. It is repeatedly asserted that Paul is writing about himself, at first hand, whereas Luke writes at second hand.

Much, therefore, is at stake in establishing that the author of Acts was the personal companion of Paul. This is to be inferred by the so-called "we" passages in Acts. Most of the Acts narrative is cast in the third person "he,"

---

10. The Pastoral Letters were directed to individuals Timothy and Titus, written ca. AD 62–65.

"they." But there are two passages in Acts written in the first person plural "we."

The first "we" passage begins in Troas and ends in Philippi in ca. AD 49 (Acts 16:10–16). The second "we" passage begins in Philippi in ca. AD 57 and narrates Paul's final journey to Palestine, his imprisonment there, and his journey to and imprisonment in Rome, a period of about five years.[11]

When readers of the Prologue to Luke-Acts (Luke 1:1–4) reach the "we" passages they naturally conclude that the author became Paul's companion throughout those passages, that author and companion are one and the same person.

Joseph Fitzmyer agrees, observing this about the "we" sources:

> They are drawn from a diary-like record that the author of Acts once kept and give evidence that he was for a time a companion of Paul.[12]

Martin Hengel reached the same conclusion:

> The remarks in the first person plural refer to the author himself. They do not go back to an earlier independent source, nor are they merely a literary convention, giving the impression that the author was an eyewitness.... "We" therefore appears in the travel narratives because Luke simply wanted to indicate that he was there.[13]

This, surely, is correct. What else could "we" in the "we" passages mean? The alternatives, that the author has employed the first person for stylistic reasons, or has reproduced "undigested" a diarist's source, seem far-fetched. We cannot overemphasize the importance of establishing this connection between Luke and Paul.

Who, then, was this author-companion? While the text of Luke-Acts does not identify him, the second century authorities—the Muratorian Canon (lines 2–8) and Irenaeus (*Adversus haereses* 3.1,1; 3.14,1)—point to Paul's friend Luke.[14]

Since (as we have argued) the author of Acts was Paul's companion for the years AD 57–62, he was contemporary with the events he narrates, including those involving Paul. He is not, therefore, *in principle*, secondary

---

11. Acts 20:5—21:18; 27:1—28:16.
12. Fitzmyer, *Luke the Theologian*, 22.
13. Hengel, *Acts and the History*, 66.
14. Col 4:14; 2 Tim 4:11; Phil 24.

to or less reliable than the person he writes about. An eyewitness of good memory and judicious perception may be an equal or better source of information than the subject himself. A wife's recollection of events involving her husband often proves more accurate than his! Since Paul's companion in the "we" passages is the author of Acts, we must allow the probability that he is a valuable source of information about Paul at that time. We assert that Acts should be regarded as an *equal primary source* with Paul for the events where Luke was part of the narrative.

We actually glean more about Paul's early life from the book of Acts than we do from Paul himself. In other words, for events concerning Paul (at least) we must not disconnect Paul from Acts as a source for his early years.

Conclusion

Thanks to the collection of Paul's letters and the narrative of Acts 13–28 we have a comprehensive account of his life story. There are parallels to this Paul-Luke nexus, for example between Cicero's letters and Plutarch's life of the great man. The big difference, however, is that Plutarch was not Cicero's companion, whereas Luke was a special friend of Paul and his companion for about five years.

Appendix: Paul's Early Life

Apart from the handful of references below, Paul himself tells his readers remarkably little about his early life, most probably because he told them about himself when he established the churches.[15]

---

15. This does not include information from his three private, so-called Pastoral Letters (Titus; 1 and 2 Timothy).

For you have heard of my former life in Judaism, how I persecuted the church of God violently and tried to destroy it. And I was advancing in Judaism beyond many of my own age among my people, so extremely zealous was I for the traditions of my fathers.	Are they Hebrews? So am I. Are they Israelites? So am I. Are they offspring of Abraham? So am I. Are they servants of Christ? I am a better one—I am talking like a madman	I myself am an Israelite, a descendant of Abraham, a member of the tribe of Benjamin.	Circumcised on the eighth day, of the people of Israel, of the tribe of Benjamin, a Hebrew of Hebrews; as to the law, a Pharisee; as to zeal, a persecutor of the church; as to righteousness under the law, blameless.
Gal 1:13–14	2 Cor 11:22–23	Rom 11:1	Phil 3:5–6

Paul provides no details about his birthplace or early life. For these we depend on the Acts of the Apostles from which we learn that his birthplace was Tarsus, that he was born a Roman citizen, and that he migrated as a teenager to Jerusalem where he became a disciple of Rabbi Gamaliel.

Three

Paul's Story 1: The First Thirty Years (AD 4–34)

As to righteousness under the law, blameless.

Phil 3:6

WE BEGIN BY LOOKING at Paul's life during his first thirty years.

Tarsus: The Childhood Years (AD 4–17)

Paul described himself as "a Jew from Tarsus, a citizen of no obscure city."[1] Tarsus was the major city in the region of Cilicia that belonged to the Roman province of Syria-Cilicia whose capital was Antioch. Tarsus was a city of the second rank, inferior to Athens in scholarship, and to Antioch in political importance.

As a "citizen" of Tarsus, Paul held a position of privilege inherited from his father. Substantial wealth, property worth the equivalent of two years wages, was needed to qualify as a citizen of Tarsus. We do not know how Paul's father or his earlier antecedents became part of the Jewish diaspora away from the land of Israel.[2]

---

1. Acts 21:39. More literally he calls himself "a Tarsian" (also: Acts 9:31). Paul's letters do not mention Tarsus, or that he was originally known as "Saul."

2. Jerome, a Christian leader from the late fourth century, stated that Paul's father was brought as a prisoner of war and slave from Gischala in Galilee but was later manumitted (Jerome, *On Illustrious Men*, 5).

Paul's Story 1: The First Thirty Years (AD 4–34)

Even more significantly Paul was *a citizen of Rome*, which he was from birth.[3] It is not known how his father was granted Roman citizenship, a rare privilege for non-Italians. Perhaps he had offered valuable service to one of the great Romans who passed through Tarsus. Some have suggested that Paul's trade as a tent maker identified the family business that had brought his father wealth and influence.[4] Had Paul's father supplied tents to a Roman army?

A Roman citizen had to register the birth of his children before a Roman magistrate, when he received a certification inscribed in wood that provided life-long proof of his citizenship.[5] It is almost certain that Paul's Roman citizenship helped him decide the cities he would visit. His right to declare, "I am a Roman citizen" (*civis romanus sum*) offered him powerful protection in Roman colonies, for example, Antioch in Pisidia, Philippi, and Corinth. In prison in Caesarea in Judea Paul's appeal to his Roman citizenship secured his right to be tried by Caesar in Rome (Acts 25:11–12; 26:32).

Tarsus was a Greek-speaking city tinged with Roman influence from the invading armies from the west that passed through Cilicia. The university in Tarsus was famous for its succession of Stoic philosophers, for example, Zeno the founder of the Stoic philosophy.

Some authorities argue that Paul underwent locally based primary level education, including instruction in letter writing and rhetoric.[6] This, it is suggested, explains Paul's skills as a preacher and letter writer.

However, as a Jew from an ultra strict Jewish family Paul is unlikely to have been greatly influenced by the philosophical or social culture in Tarsus.

Many years later Paul recalled his earliest years in Tarsus:

> Circumcised on the eighth day,
> of the people of Israel,
> of the tribe of Benjamin,
> a Hebrew of Hebrews.[7]

Paul's family belonged to the tribe of Benjamin, the tribe of Israel's first king, Saul, after whom Paul was named. Three times in Rom 16 Paul

---

3. Acts 22:28.
4. Tents were then made of leather.
5. Sherwin-White, *Roman Citizenship*, 6.
6. Murphy-O'Connor, *Paul*, 46–51.
7. Phil 3:5–6.

refers positively to six named persons as "kinsmen," which probably means that they were members of the same tribe as Paul, and may have lived in Tarsus. After Paul's conversion he returned to Tarsus for almost a decade (AD 37–47) where his family and "kinsmen" may have looked after him.

A "Hebrew of Hebrews" suggests that Paul's family were deeply committed members of the Jewish community in Tarsus. Their lives would have revolved around Sabbath attendance of the synagogue, which also provided their social network. As a citizen of Tarsus and as a Roman citizen it is likely that Paul's father was a prominent and leading member of the Jewish community of Tarsus.

Although Tarsus had a long history as a city of Greek culture it is unlikely that an ultra-conservative Jew would have exposed his son to any kind of public education. Rather, his father would have employed a domestic tutor and arranged for his son to attend the synagogue school (from five years of age).

This would help explain why Paul's writings have no clear echoes of Homer or Plato and betray limited sophistication in Greek rhetorical forms, which we would expect had he attended one of the philosophical schools in Tarsus. His letters have some allusions from the cultural world of the Greeks, but Paul may have come across these in popularized forms as an adult in the course of his travels.[8] Rather, his writings are permeated with the language and ideas of the Greek Bible (known as the Septuagint).[9]

"As to Zeal, a Persecutor of the Church"

Paul saw himself, as other people saw him, as a man of "zeal." The young émigré from Tarsus, a student in the most prominent rabbinic academy, had earned himself a reputation that was for him a source of pride.

The word translated "zeal" is also understood as "jealousy," jealousy for the reputation of the Lord. The young scholar knew of Phinehas's zeal in spearing the Hebrew man in coitus with the Midianite woman, and of Elijah's "zeal" for the Lord in killing the prophets of Baal. He would have known also the words of Mattathias, father of Judas Maccabeus, "Let

---

8. E.g., Paul's "bad company corrupts good morals" (1 Cor 15:33) occurs in the poet Menander's play, *Thais* (fragment 218). It may, however, have become a popular maxim.

9. The Hebrew Bible was translated into Greek in Alexandria in the third century BC and, according to legend, by seventy scholars, hence its name in Latin, *Septuaginta*. In his letters Paul usually quotes from or alludes to the Septuagint.

everyone who has *zeal* for the law . . . follow me,"¹⁰ whereupon the clan patriarch slaughtered the fellow Jew who stepped forward to worship the Greek gods.

The fundamental thing about "zeal" was that it did something (usually violent) to defend the honor of the Lord. Paul expressed his "zeal" in his attack on the followers of the false-messiah, Jesus. His disciple Stephen had criticized the twin pillars of Judaism, the temple and the law.

> For you have heard of my former life in Judaism, how I persecuted the church of God violently and tried to destroy it. And I was advancing in Judaism beyond many of my own age among my people so extremely *zealous* was I for the traditions of my fathers.[11]

> I am a Jew, born in Tarsus in Cilicia, but brought up in this city, educated at the feet of Gamaliel according to the strict manner of the law of our fathers, being *zealous* for God as all of you are this day. I persecuted this Way to the death.[12]

"Zeal," then, was a religious disposition, a mindset that issued in action. "Zeal" for the Lord burst out at particular moments of crisis, for example, when a group of young Pharisees tore down the effigy of a Roman eagle on the gate of the temple, and were burned alive for their trouble.[13]

During the Roman siege of Jerusalem a faction known as the "zealots" arose. It was a protest movement by lesser priests against the high priest's collaboration with the Roman authorities. Its passion was zeal for the purity of the temple. This group perished during the final Roman onslaught upon the temple in AD 70.

Paul was called a "zealot" and took pride in that reputation, but it would be anachronistic to think of him as belonging to a movement that arose three decades after his conversion. It was a disposition associated with *individuals*. For example, one of Jesus' disciples was known as Simon the Zealot.[14]

After the Lord's dramatic intervention outside Damascus we continue to witness Paul's zeal, but it was now immediately and radically redirected.

---

10. 1 Macc 2:27.
11. Gal 1:13–14.
12. Acts 22:3–5.
13. Josephus, *Jewish War* 1. 648–53 (Loeb).
14. Luke 6:15; Acts 1:13.

> *Immediately* he proclaimed Jesus in the synagogues [of Damascus], saying, "He is the Son of God."[15]

Some years later Paul responded to the Corinthians' welcome of visiting teachers who were proclaiming *"another* Jesus . . . a *different* gospel." Paul told them, "I feel a divine *jealousy* ['zeal'] for you, for I betrothed you to one husband, to present you as a pure virgin to Christ."[16] Paul's passionate and single-minded concern was that the church in Corinth remained faithful to the apostolic Jesus.

Paul's Name

The book of Acts calls him "Saul" until his encounter with the Roman proconsul of Cyprus, Sergius *Paulus*.[17] It seems that Paul himself deliberately took the name "Paul" at that time, in honor of a famous Roman.

As a Roman citizen Paul would have had a clan name and a forename, neither of which we know. We only know him by the very Jewish name "Saul." He may have adopted the Roman name "Paul" because he was increasingly active in the cities of the Roman Empire.

Jerusalem: The Formative Years (AD 17–34)

Important as his years in Tarsus would have been for Paul, it was in Jerusalem where his most profound formation occurred.

Years later when Paul made what would be his final visit to Jerusalem (in AD 57) he spoke these words to the gathered crowd:

> I am a Jew, born in Tarsus in Cilicia, but brought up in this city, at the feet of Gamaliel, educated according to the strict manner of the laws of our fathers.[18]

Later Paul explained his years in Jerusalem to King Herod Agrippa II:

> My manner of life from my youth spent from the beginning among my own nation and at Jerusalem, is known to all the Jews.[19]

15. Acts 9:21.
16. 2 Cor 11:2.
17. Acts 13:9.
18. Acts 22:3.
19. Acts 26:4.

Paul's Story 1: The First Thirty Years (AD 4–34)

When we combine these statements the following picture of Paul emerges. From his "youth" (12 or 13 years) he was "brought up" in Jerusalem and "educated" as a Pharisee by Rabbi Gamaliel. The strictness of his early years in Tarsus continued in Jerusalem as a disciple of the Master-Pharisee, Gamaliel.

On the assumption of his date of birth in AD 4 it seems Paul came from Tarsus to Jerusalem "from his youth" in AD 16 where he remained until AD 34.[20] In ca. AD 59 there is a reference to Paul's sister and nephew residing in Jerusalem,[21] which suggests that several members of Paul's family had also come to live in Jerusalem.

Was Paul Married?

Although in ca. AD 55 Paul referred to himself as "unmarried"[22] his Greek word (*agamos*) could mean "widower." It is thought that Jews at that time were expected to marry, although there are few contemporary texts to confirm this. Jewish tradition declared a man fit for the bride chamber at eighteen years.[23] Paul may have been married at about that age but widowed or divorced during his years in Jerusalem, but there is no clear evidence.

A Pharisee

Paul declared that he was "as to the law, a Pharisee,"[24] which implies that there were *other* approaches to the interpretation and application of the Law of Moses. Josephus, who had been a Pharisee, confirmed that impression.

> The Pharisees are considered the most accurate interpreters of the laws, and hold the position of the leading sect.[25]

Thus, there were other interpreters of the laws and other sects, the Qumran community, for example.

---

20. Unnik, "Tarsus or Jerusalem," 259–320, argues that Paul was brought from Tarsus to Jerusalem as a small child. So, too, Hengel, *Pre-Christian Paul*, 22–23.
21. Acts 23:16.
22. 1 Cor 7:7, 9, 38, 40; 9:4.
23. Mishnah *Aboth* 5.21.
24. Phil 3:5.
25. Josephus, *Jewish War* 2.162.

The Pharisee movement originated two centuries earlier in reaction to the beliefs and values of the surrounding Greek empires, the Ptolemaic to the south (based in Alexandria) and the Seleucid to the north (based in Antioch in Syria). The Pharisees (a word possibly meaning "Separatists") evolved from a devout group known as Hasideans, the "holy ones." By the era of Jesus, the Pharisees were organized closed communities (called *haburot*) where learned scholars instructed them in the interpretation of laws of God.

The Pharisees' goal was to make all the people of Israel as pure as the priests were at the time of their two-week long temple duties. To that end the Pharisees acted like "religious police," reinforcing the religious calendar, Sabbath keeping, dietary law, fasting, tithing, and the purity washings. This is the role we see them employing in the Gospel of Mark in relation to Jesus' table fellowship with "tax collectors and sinners,"[26] to his disciples' failure to fast,[27] to his calculated breaking of the Sabbath,[28] and to his disciples' failure to ceremoniously wash their hands.[29]

According to the Talmud (codified many years later) the Pharisees applied considerable moral pressure on the people.

> If Israel were to keep two Sabbaths according to the rules, they would immediately be redeemed.[30]

Philo the Jewish philosopher from Alexandria doesn't mention the name "Pharisee" in this next quotation, but there is little doubt he was referring to them. Philo's words confirm the severity of the Pharisees toward law-breakers.

> There are thousands who have their eyes on [God], full of zeal for the laws of the ancestral institutions, merciless to any who subvert them.[31]

The Pharisees' sphere of influence was the synagogue where they excluded people they classified as impure—tax collectors and those they

---

26. Mark 2:15.
27. Mark 2:18.
28. Mark 2:23—3:6.
29. Mark 7:1–2.
30. *bSanhedrin* 97.a
31. Philo, *Special Laws* 2.253.

Paul's Story 1: The First Thirty Years (AD 4–34)

called "sinners," that is, prostitutes and others who pursued despised trades (for example, herdsmen, tanners, carters, bath attendants, physicians).[32]

The absolute standards and strictures of the Pharisees inevitably created the underclass, "sinners," whom we meet in the pages of the Synoptic Gospels. From the Gospel of John we read that the blind man and his parents were fearful that the Pharisees would excommunicate them from the synagogue.[33] To be banned from the synagogue amounted to being driven from mainstream society to the underclass, with dire economic consequences.

The Pharisees, by contrast with the tax collectors, refused to be baptized by John.[34] They were indignant that Jesus welcomed the tax collectors and ate with them.[35] Since the Pharisees' goal was to coerce Israel to comply with the laws of purity, they would have regarded Jesus as a major obstacle to that goal. Jesus broke those very laws and encouraged his disciples to do the same.

For his part, Jesus condemned the Pharisees for hypocrisy,[36] for social pretentiousness, for lack of compassion toward the needy,[37] for greed,[38] for a self-justifying spirit that lacked humility before God,[39] and for willfully refusing the invitation of Jesus.

As a Pharisee Paul was as devoted to the laws of Moses as he was to defending the honor of God. The Hellenist Jew Stephen, disciple of Jesus, denounced both the laws of Moses and the temple.[40] Paul, who wrote "as to zeal a persecutor of the church,"[41] was complicit in the stoning of Stephen.

Ironically, after the resurrection, there were Pharisees who had become Christian believers, but who were as opposed to Paul as they had

---

32. See further Jeremias, *Jerusalem in the Time of Jesus*, 303–12.

33. John 9:22—"His parents said these things because they feared the Jews, for the Jews had already agreed that if anyone should confess Jesus to be Christ, he was to be put out of the synagogue (*aposynagōgos*)." The context makes clear that here "Jews" equals Pharisees (John 9:13–16).

34. Luke 7:30.
35. Luke 5:30; 7:34; 15:1–2.
36. Luke 11:39, 42; 12:1.
37. Luke 11:43; 14:7, 12–14.
38. Luke 6:14.
39. Luke 10:29.
40. Acts 6:11, 13–14.
41. Phil 3:6.

been to Jesus.[42] It was the spirit of the Pharisee that inspired waves of the proselytizing counter-mission against Paul, in Galatia, Syria and Cilicia, and Achaia.

Paul under Gamaliel

Gamaliel appears on one other occasion in the book of Acts, where the Council of the Jews were about to execute the apostles.

> But a Pharisee in the council named Gamaliel, a teacher of the law held in honor by all the people, stood up and ordered the men to be put outside for a while.[43]

Gamaliel was a member of the Sanhedrin, a teacher of the law and universally respected. Such was his authority that *he* directed the disciples to go outside the chamber. His judgement saved the lives of the apostles.

Gamaliel is referred to many times within the Jewish tradition. According to the *Mishnah*, the two main interpreters of the law were Hillel and Shammai. Hillel was especially important because it was believed that he had received the wisdom that God gave initially to Moses at Mt. Sinai. Gamaliel was either the son or grandson of Hillel and his successor in that revered line of scholarship. According to the *Mishnah*, "When Rabbi Gamaliel died the glory of the Torah ceased, and purity and abstinence died."[44]

Paul does not mention Gamaliel in his letters but he confirms the Acts' version of his progress as a scholar.

> I was advancing in Judaism beyond many of my own age among my people, so extremely zealous was I for the traditions of my fathers.[45]

From the time of his arrival in Jerusalem Paul's emerging prominence was noticed in high places. It is no surprise that he argued against the new

---

42. Acts 15:5—"Some believers who belonged to the party of the Pharisees rose up and said, 'It is necessary to circumcise them [gentiles] and to order them to keep the Law of Moses.'"

43. Acts 5:34.

44. Mishnah *Sotah* 9:15. The Talmud reference to a Gamaliel who had five hundred young men in his "house" who studied the Torah and five hundred who studied Greek wisdom (*b. B. Qam* 83a) probably relates to another, later Gamaliel.

45. Gal 1:14.

Paul's Story 1: The First Thirty Years (AD 4-34)

sect of the Nazarenes and figured significantly in the stoning of Stephen and in the subsequent attacks on the disciples.

Rabbi Paul in Jerusalem

As well as Greek, Paul also spoke Aramaic, the other main language of the Jews in Palestine.[46] As a scholar in the Pharisee tradition he also knew classical Hebrew, the language of the Bible. From his letters we know that he wrote grammatically correct Greek, with access to a large vocabulary. It is possible that Paul the Roman citizen also knew Latin.

One striking aspect of Paul's letters is his "sovereign treatment"[47] of the Greek Old Testament. His confident knowledge would have begun through his attendance at the synagogue school in Tarsus and have developed during his years in Jerusalem.

Luke intends us to understand that Paul visited the Greek-speaking ("Hellenist") synagogues in Jerusalem where he heard the radical Christian preaching of Stephen.[48] It is possible that the so-called "Cilician" synagogue in Jerusalem[49] was Paul's spiritual home where he may have been one of the synagogue teachers.

The Jerusalem Context: AD 17-34

Paul's years in Jerusalem (AD 17-34) belonged to the period when Judea was for the first time a Roman province (as from AD 6). Roman troops were now visible evidence that Judea was occupied by a foreign power.

In AD 26 things took an ominous turn. The emperor Tiberius handed the control of the empire to his Praetorian prefect, Sejanus, who in turn appointed Pontius Pilate as military prefect of Judea. It appears that Sejanus hated the Jews[50] and sent Pilate to Judea to destabilize the Jewish people.[51]

---

46. Acts 22:3, where "the Hebrew language" means Aramaic.
47. Hengel, *Pre-Christian Paul*, 35.
48. Acts 6:9-14.
49. Acts 6:9.
50. Philo, *Flaccus* 1.1; *Embassy to Gaius* 159-160. See Smallwood, "Some Notes on the Jews," 325. It is possible that Sejanus harbored hopes of a personal cult (Tacitus *Annals* 3.72; 4.2, 272; Suetonius *Tiberius* 48, 65; Dio Cassius lviii.2, 4; 5.7).
51. See Doyle, "Pilate's Career," 190-93; Maier, "Sejanus, Pilate," 3-13; Maier, "Episode of the Golden Roman Shields," 109-21.

Pilate provoked incident after incident to upset the Jews, to provide him with the excuse to unleash his soldiers on the crowds.[52]

In the year AD 28 Jerusalem and Judea were deeply stirred by the appearance of the prophet John the Baptist in Transjordan and soon after by a charismatic Galilean rabbi, Jesus from Nazareth in Galilee. Large crowds from Judea attended John, but multitudes from the whole land of Israel and the adjoining Greek principalities also flocked to hear Jesus.

Paul the Pharisee would have been deeply conscious of and concerned about the appearance of John and Jesus and the multitudes that gathered to hear them. The Pharisees saw themselves as having spiritual oversight of the people. But many were gathering to hear the wisdom of these new leaders.

Paul does not indicate in his letters that he had directly heard either John or Jesus, but his words to the Galatians that he had "publicly portrayed Jesus Christ as crucified"[53] may mean that he had witnessed the crucifixion.

Paul's Attempt to Destroy Christianity (AD 34)

Paul wrote that he "persecuted the church of God violently and tried to destroy it" and that he had "tried to destroy the faith."[54] Why did Paul attempt to destroy "the church of God" and "the [Christian] faith"?

Paul's violent attack on the original disciples in Jerusalem is in contrast to the earlier, less violent attack on them by the temple authorities. The chief priests punished the apostles for preaching that the resurrected Jesus was the Messiah, but their punishments were intended to deter this preaching rather than to destroy the disciples. This was because in other ways the first Christians were observant Jews, including regularly attending the temple at the hours of prayer.[55] So far as the Jewish leadership was concerned the disciples were part of an outspoken Jewish sect, but one that could perhaps be moderated.

All that changed, however, when a subgroup of the disciples who were known as "Hellenists" became prominent. These were Greek-speaking Jews who had settled in Jerusalem in the recent decades. Their spokesman,

---

52. Josephus, *Jewish War* 2.169–177; *Jewish Antiquities* 18.55–62; cf. Luke 13:1; Mark 15:7. For Philo's very negative report on Pilate see *Embassy to Gaius* 299, 302.

53. Gal 3:1.

54. Gal 1:13, 21.

55. Acts 3:1; cf. 10:3.

Paul's Story 1: The First Thirty Years (AD 4–34)

Stephen, actually preached against the temple, referring to it as "made by hands," a hand-made idol! According to Stephen, the Jews had come to regard the temple as a god. It is likely that Stephen knew of Jesus' reference to the temple as a "den of robbers," prophesying that it would be wholly destroyed in the coming days.

The "Hebrew" apostles did not attack the temple, but Stephen the Greek Jew did, and this aroused the ire of the young, precocious Pharisee, Paul. In effect, by attacking the temple Stephen was also attacking the priests and the sacrifices, the whole fabric of Israel's atonement beliefs.

Paul stated that he had attempted to annihilate the newly born Christian church, but gives no details, though the book of Acts does. First, Paul was complicit in the stoning of Stephen. Then immediately afterward, with the permission of the high priest, he set about "ravaging the church . . . and entering house after house . . . dragged off men and women and committed them to prison."[56]

Acts also reports that Paul said, "I not only locked up many of the saints in prison . . . but when they were put to death . . . I cast my vote against them. . . . I punished them in the synagogues and tried to make them blaspheme."[57] Paul directly said about himself that, "as to zeal," he was "a *persecutor* of the church."[58]

Ironically, the brutal thirty-nine lashes Paul administered to the disciples in the synagogues of Jerusalem he also received as a disciple of Jesus no less than five times.[59]

Damascus: The Turning Point (AD 34)

The hinge around which Paul's life story turns occurred outside the ancient city of Damascus.

Paul's violent attack on the church in Jerusalem drove its members (except the apostles) from the city. The Jewish believers (who were referred to as "Hebrews") dispersed throughout the three regions of Israel—Judea, Samaria, and Galilee. Like "scattered seed" they "took root" and became "churches" throughout the whole land.

---

56. Acts 8:3; cf. 9:1, 13, 21.
57. Acts 26:10–11.
58. Phil 3:6.
59. 2 Cor 11:24.

The "Hellenist" disciples, however, mostly left Israel altogether. Some travelled north along the coast and finished in the great metropolis, Antioch in Syria. Others, however, escaped to the northeast, to Damascus, just beyond the borders of Israel.

Hearing of this, the persecutor secured authority from the high priest to travel to Damascus to seize these disciples and bring them back to face trial and punishment in Jerusalem.[60]

Paul knew that Jesus had been crucified, which was proof that he was a false messiah. The book of Deuteronomy states that a man who has committed a crime punishable by death is to be "hanged on a tree" (i.e., a pole, or gallows) and that after death such "a hanged man is cursed by God." The body of the hanged man must not remain unburied overnight.[61]

The temple authorities had tried Jesus, found him guilty of claiming to be the Messiah, and handed him over to the Romans to be crucified, after which Jesus was hung "on a tree." For Paul, Jesus' "hanging on a tree" was proof that God had cursed him. The preaching of his disciple Stephen against the temple was further evidence that his leader, Jesus, was the accursed of God.

As a "zealot," one for whom the honor of God was uppermost, Paul felt duty-bound to destroy the movement founded by Jesus.

Damascus: The Light, the Voice

The bright light flashed around him and the voice called out, "Saul, Saul, why are you persecuting me?" To Paul's question, "who are you?" the voice replied, "I am Jesus whom you are persecuting."[62] In persecuting his followers, Paul was persecuting Jesus himself. Paul the Pharisee was no guilt-ridden Martin Luther, longing for the release of a clear conscience. Paul's motivation as persecutor was not personal guilt but outrage at the disciples' blasphemous proclamation that the crucified—therefore accursed—pretender was the Christ of God.

What from Paul's viewpoint actually happened on the Damascus Road?

---

60. Acts 9:1–2.
61. Deut 21:23; cf. Josh 8:26–27.
62. Acts 9:4.

Paul's Story 1: The First Thirty Years (AD 4–34)

First, God opened Paul's eyes about Jesus. He later wrote, "God revealed *his Son* to (*en*, "in") me" and "God shone in" my "heart."[63] Only God spoke from the glory of heaven, as he had to Moses.[64] In speaking from the brightness of heaven, Jesus revealed to Paul that he was the Son of God. Suddenly Paul understood how the *crucified* one was now the *glorified* One. His crucifixion was expiatory; he bore God's curse but he bore it *for others*, on their behalf. It was then, as Paul said, that he "received mercy."[65]

At the same time Paul the Pharisee grasped the radical truth that righteousness with God was not through keeping the Law of Moses, as he had believed, but through a faith relationship with the Son of God.

Secondly, it was from that time Paul was "in Christ," irrevocably joined and united to Christ. This would mean a profound turnabout within the depths of Paul's being, nothing less than a "conversion." Referring to himself as the paradigm convert he declared, "If anyone is in Christ he is a new creation. The old has passed away; behold the new has come."[66] God converted Paul, radically changed his understanding, his worldview, and his life's direction.

Thirdly, closely connected with this was God's "call" to proclaim his Son among the gentiles, that is, to extend the blessings of the divine covenant to the non-Jewish world, in fulfillment of the promise to Abraham that "in" him [i.e., Christ] "all the nations of the world shall be blessed."[67] Paul was to be God's apostle to bring the blessings of God, as promised to Abraham, to the whole world. Nothing was so radical to the young Pharisee as God's commission to include non-Jews in the sacred covenant independently of the Jewish Law.

Thus, at least three things occurred outside Damascus: as a man "in Christ" Paul was converted from living for himself, to living for Christ;[68] he was "called" by God to preach Christ among the gentiles; and his message was to be Christ-centered and Law-free.

The main pieces of the jigsaw fell into place outside Damascus. Before the heavenly revelation Paul had known some things at least about Jesus of Nazareth, especially that he had been crucified. He knew firsthand that

---

63. Gal 1:16.
64. Exod 34:29–35.
65. 2 Cor 4:1.
66. 2 Cor 5:17.
67. Gen 12:3.
68. 2 Cor 5:15.

Jesus' followers preached against the laws of Moses and the temple and its sacrifices and, furthermore, that when punished his disciples had been non-vengeful.

In Damascus, after "the revelation" from heaven, he would learn more in the course of preparation for his baptism, for example, about the Holy Spirit.[69] Later again, Paul would be instructed about Jesus from the lips of Peter and James.[70]

But the light and the voice outside Damascus fitted the pieces together in a way that permanently changed Paul's life. Thirty years later he would say, simply, "Christ Jesus seized me."[71]

The Risen Lord's confrontation of Paul outside Damascus in the year AD 34 converted the attempted destroyer of the faith to become its most effective advocate. It was no merely subjective vision. Paul saw the light and heard the voice of Jesus; and his companions also saw the light and heard the voice but saw no one.[72] But God also uniquely revealed himself within the depths of Paul's life. He wrote that "God had revealed his Son *in* me," "shone his light *in* my heart," and made Paul his "new creation."[73] What happened outside Damascus was so profound and permanent that it changed Paul from within.

Many times Paul referred to his life in "before and after" terms, as if his former life ended at Damascus and his new life began at Damascus. His use of completed action verb tenses is telling, for example: he was "*set apart* for the gospel of God"; he "*received* grace and apostleship"; "necessity is *laid* on me. . . . I am *entrusted* with a stewardship"; he "*received* mercy."[74] He speaks of Christ having "seized" him and of being a "new creation."[75] These and more subtle references, of which there are many, point to that moment outside Damascus when Paul's life underwent radical change of understanding and of life's direction.

---

69. Acts 9:18.
70. Gal 1:18–19.
71. Phil 3:12.
72. Acts 9:7; 22:9.
73. Gal 1:6; 2 Cor 4:6; 5:17.
74. Rom 1:1, 5; 1 Cor 9:17
75. Phil 3:12; 2 Cor 5:17.

Four

Paul's Story 2: His Second Thirty Years (AD 34–65)

Damascus and Arabia (AD 34–36)

Paul, temporarily blinded by the bright light, was led into Damascus where a disciple named Ananias baptized him (probably in the Barada River) and brought him to other disciples in the city. Astonishingly, Paul immediately preached in the synagogues in Damascus that Jesus is the Son of God and the Christ.[1] Yet this sense of urgency was deeply part of Paul, whether as a persecutor or as a preacher. The Jews in Damascus reacted strongly and forced Paul to flee from the city, and not for the last time.

Paul did not return to Jerusalem, but "went away into Arabia,"[2] that is, into the Nabatean kingdom. Nabatea, whose capital was Petra near the Gulf of Aqaba, was a desert region to the east of Gaulanitis, Perea, and the Dead Sea. The Nabateans' prosperity came from the collection of taxes from traders passing through their territory and from their expertise in desert farming.

Paul's visit to "Arabia" probably extended for more than two years because his two visits to Damascus were quite brief. So far as we know Paul travelled there alone. Did he reach as far south as Petra? We do not know,

---

1. Acts 9:19–22.
2. Gal 1:17.

but it is not unlikely. It was in "Arabia" that Paul first obeyed God's call for him to proclaim God's Son "among the gentiles."

Then Paul "returned again to Damascus"[3] where, some time later, the "consul" under King Aretas (9 BC–AD 40) was guarding the city in order to seize him. It is not clear at that time whether Damascus was under the control of the Romans or Herod Antipas, the Tetrarch of Galilee. Whoever it was, those in control recognized an ethnic head of the Nabatean community living in Damascus, an official who was called a "consul" (Greek, *ethnarchēs*).[4]

We conclude that Paul had stirred up trouble beforehand by preaching Christ in Nabatea. As a Jew, Paul would also have been unwelcome in the Arabian kingdom. Herod Antipas, the tetrarch of Galilee, had humiliated Phasaelis, daughter of Aretas, by his adulterous liaison with Herodias, his sister-in-law. Aretas later successfully invaded Galilee to punish Herod Antipas.

Once again Paul was forced to flee from Damascus. To this day there are still dwellings built into the upper parts of the city walls, making the stories of Paul's escapes in a basket down the walls quite credible.

Paul Returns to Jerusalem: Stays with Peter, Meets James (AD 37)

Three years after the Damascus Road conversion Paul the former persecutor returned to Jerusalem where he "remained with" Peter for fifteen days and also "saw" James, brother of the Lord. This sequence implies that Peter was the leader of the community and James the next most senior leader. These were private meetings but Paul also met with the other apostles in Jerusalem.

It is critically important to note the significance of these meetings between Paul and the leaders, Peter and James. There is no hint of hostility by these apostles toward the ex-Pharisee who had attempted to destroy the church. This implies that they accepted the reality of his conversion and of God's "call" for him to preach to the non-Jews. It is probable that Peter and James approved of and endorsed the content of his Christ-centered, law-free gospel preaching.

---

3. Gal 1:17.
4. 2 Cor 11:31.

Paul's Story 2: His Second Thirty Years (AD 34–65)

Equally these meetings gave Paul the priceless opportunity to hear about Jesus' early life from James, his brother, and about the Lord's teaching and miracles from his companion and eyewitness, Peter. Paul later delivered to the churches the traditions he had received, for example about the Last Supper and the Easter tradition.[5] Almost certainly Paul learned these traditions during this visit to Jerusalem.

Paul began to preach in Jerusalem, as he had done in Damascus and Arabia. Once again he stirred up such hostility that he was forced to flee. He returned to his home province, Syria-Cilicia, where he remained for the next ten years.

In the Regions of Syria and Cilicia (AD 37–47)

One of the strangest features of the Acts of the Apostles is that the author devotes so little narrative to the next ten years of Paul's life.[6] The book of Acts takes Paul back to Tarsus and later from Tarsus to Antioch, with no information about the decade in those cities and their localities. Luke devotes only three verses to the entire decade.[7] It is understandable that these should be called Paul's "unknown years."[8]

Why would Luke be silent about this lengthy phase of the life of Paul, who is his chief focus of interest? The answer relates to the author's overall concern, which is to narrate how the message about Christ made its way from Jerusalem westward *to Rome*, the capital of the gentile world. Luke devotes a significant expanse of text—seventy-seven verses—to relate Peter's travels to the Roman Cornelius and his subsequent baptism.[9] Paul, however, was more or less stationary throughout these ten years, in Syria and Cilicia.

Despite Luke's silence we have some vital information from these years.

---

5. 1 Cor 11:23–25; 15:3–7.
6. Acts 9:23–30; 11:25–30; 12:25.
7. Acts 9:30; 11:25–26.
8. Hengel and Schwemer, *Between Damascus and Antioch*.
9. Acts 9:32—11:18.

Preaching "the Faith" in Syria and Cilicia

Paul himself refers to vigorous preaching in Syria and Cilicia during the years AD 37–47.

> Then I went into the regions of Syria and Cilicia. And I was still unknown in person to the churches of Judea that are in Christ. They only were hearing it said, "He who used to persecute us is now preaching the faith he once attempted to destroy." And they glorified God because of me.[10]

The stellar effects of Paul's preaching in "the regions of Syria and Cilicia"[11] came to the attention of "the churches of Christ in Judea." That Paul proclaimed the Christian "faith" in the regions of Syria and Cilicia is evidence that Paul did not merely *take refuge* in Tarsus (with his "kinsmen"?).

Gentile Churches in Syria and Cilicia

We discover, almost by accident, that there were *gentile* churches in Syria and Cilicia. The Jerusalem Council in AD 49 issued a letter to "the gentiles in Antioch and Syria and Cilicia":

> The brothers, both the apostles and the elders, to the brothers who are of the gentiles in Antioch and Syria and Cilicia.[12]

> And [Paul] went through Syria and Cilicia, strengthening the churches.[13]

---

10. Gal 1:21–24.

11. Cilicia is a boomerang shaped region that wraps around the northeast corner of the Mediterranean. The large coastal plain ("flat Cilicia"—*Kilikia Pedias*) is hedged in at the east and north by the Taurus Mountains ("rugged Cilicia"—*Kilikia Tracheia*) and to the east by the Syrian desert. Three rivers—the Cydnus, the Sarus, and the Pyramus—water the Cilician plain. Pompey's military expedition 67–64 BC began the process of Romanization when Cilicia with parts of Phrygia were formed into a province. From the time of Paul's birth and throughout his years of return to Tarsus, Cilicia had been joined to Syria as a province, whose capital was Antioch. Vespasian later made Cilicia a separate province (in AD 72).

12. Acts 15:22–23.

13. Acts 15:41.

When we combine these texts we catch a glimpse of *gentile* brothers and sisters and of *gentile* churches in Syria and Cilicia. Paul had not been idle during his years in his home province.

Synagogue Beatings

Writing in AD 56, Paul informed the Corinthians of his missionary sufferings, including repeated punishment within the synagogues.

> Five times I received at the hands of the Jews the forty lashes less one.[14]

Many authorities locate these synagogue beatings during Paul's so-called "unknown years" in Syria and Cilicia.[15] Since Luke describes Paul's later westward missions in detail we would have expected him to mention these floggings had they occurred then.

Paul had been present in a synagogue, or more probably a number of synagogues, to warrant these severe beatings. But what offence or offences had he committed?

Paul was guilty of blasphemy for denying the saving power of the Law of Moses and the necessity of circumcision for non-Jewish converts. Paul taught that faith in Christ was the only way to eternal life with God. For this serious "sin" Paul could have been cast out of Judaism. However, there was the option of submitting to the thirty-nine lashes as an alternative to excommunication from the Jewish faith. Paul wanted to be able to preach to Jews so he chose to remain a Jew by taking this very severe beating no less than five times.

If the five synagogue beatings were confined within the ten "unknown years," that would indicate that Paul engaged in synagogue ministry throughout those years. Since, as we have noted, Paul had established gentile churches throughout those years, it raises the likelihood of a connection between those beatings and the creation of these gentile churches. The synagogues beat Paul because he preached a circumcision-free gospel to synagogue-based gentiles, known as God-fearers. It appears that Paul subsequently built these gentile churches from God-fearers to whom Paul had reached in the synagogues and for whom he was repeatedly beaten.

---

14. 2 Cor 11:24.

15. See e.g., Barrett, *Commentary on the Second Epistle*: "the floggings will probably go back to the earliest period of his apostolic work" (297).

Revelation of the Lord and the "Thorn for the Flesh"[16]

It was during his decade in Syria and Cilicia that Paul had the double experience of a revelation of the Lord and God's gift of the thorn.

> I know a man in Christ who fourteen years ago was caught up to the third heaven . . . to keep me from being too elated by the surpassing greatness of the revelations, a thorn was given me in the flesh.[17]

Paul wrote this letter in AD 57 so that his rapture to the third heaven and the onset of the thorn occurred in AD 43, that is, during his years in Syria-Cilicia.

Paul was elated by this experience but, as it were, brought down to earth by the "thorn," which may have been some form of physical disability that remained with him from that time.

Paul's Unknown Years

The "unknown years" represented a considerable time span in which, based on sparse referencing in Acts, we might assume had been unproductive for Paul. However, Luke has probably given an unintended impression of Paul's inactivity during those years since his concern was to direct attention on the Jerusalem-to-Rome narrative.

When we look carefully at Acts, Galatians, and 2 Corinthians we find strong hints that Paul was anything but inactive at that time.

Paul had preached so vigorously in Syria and Cilicia that news of this reached distant Judea. He had attempted to win God-fearers to allegiance to Christ and, it appears, was flogged repeatedly for declaring that faith in Christ not "works of the law" was the only true route to "life." Paul had gathered these converts into gentile churches. The undefined "thorn" became part of his life's experience during those years.

---

16. There is no "in" in Paul's original text, but the dative case suggesting "for" the flesh, that is, as an assault on Paul's whole physical being.

17. 2 Cor 12:2, 7.

Paul's Story 2: His Second Thirty Years (AD 34-65)

Westward Missionary Extension: The Jerusalem Meeting (AD 47)

Paul spent the last years in Syria-Cilicia in the metropolis, Antioch, where he shared in the leadership of the church with Barnabas. These men reached the conclusion that the time had come to take the Christian message westward, beginning at the adjoining province, Galatia.

Neither the book of Acts nor Paul's letters tell why they made that decision at that time, so that we are left to guess the reason or reasons. Was it because the church in Antioch, composed as it was of Jews and gentiles, gave the men the vision of a growing number of such "mixed" churches spreading westward from Syria-Cilicia? Was it the growing conviction that the Jews had "hardened" their rejection of Jesus as Messiah[18] that led Paul to believe God was now opening a special door of opportunity to the gentiles?

Whatever the reason the two men, accompanied by the gentile Titus, visited Jerusalem seeking the endorsement of the three Jerusalem "pillars," James, Cephas, and John.[19] Titus was important as a demonstration of the success of the church in Antioch in producing a true believer among the gentiles. Titus, the gentile believer, was also an example of the future direction of the missionary movement headed by Barnabas and Paul.

James, Cephas, and John endorsed Paul's missionary message, blocked any attempt to have Titus circumcised, and gave their agreement to the delegates of the church in Antioch going intentionally to the gentiles.

Missions in Cyprus, Pisidia, and Lycaonia: Acts 13-14 (AD 47-48)

Following prayer and fasting the church in Antioch dispatched Barnabas and Paul for the mission to gentiles that had been endorsed in Jerusalem. They were accompanied by John Mark, a cousin of Barnabas, as an "assistant" to the two leaders.

They travelled first by ship from Seleucia in Syria to Salamis in Cyprus. Crossing the island to Paphos they engaged with a magician, Elymas, who was an attendant of Sergius Paulus, the Roman governor. His official title "proconsul" indicates that he had previously been a consul in Rome, one

---

18. See Rom 11:25-32.
19. Gal 2:1-9.

of the two most senior members of the Roman Senate. External evidence points to him belonging to a distinguished and notable Roman family.

Paul's miraculous ministry to Elymas led to the conversion of Sergius Paulus. Luke then adds briefly, "Saul, who is also Paul," explaining why from that moment he refers to the apostle only by the name Paul. The author does not explain why Saul then began to use another name, but it may have been because he wanted to honor this famous Roman, Sergius *Paulus*, and recognizing that a Jewish name would be a hindrance in his new missionary thrust into the Roman world.

The three men then went by sea to the coast of Pamphylia up the Kestros River to the important river port, Perga. Rather dramatically John Mark parted company with Paul and Barnabas and returned to Jerusalem, although Luke does not explain why. Was it because Paul had assumed leadership over Barnabas, the cousin of John Mark? Or was it because John Mark had not anticipated the degree to which Paul was seeking to win gentiles for the faith of the Messiah?

Whatever the reason, the young man went back to Jerusalem. His return may have been the source of the news in Jerusalem of the Antioch-based mission into the gentile world. Paul's letter to the Galatians reports that a circumcision-based counter-mission went from Jerusalem to the Galatian churches that Paul and Barnabas had established, seeking to complement Paul's teaching by urging gentiles to adopt Jewish "works of the law." Was John Mark the unintended source of information that led to this counter-mission?

The two men did not stop in Perga but went directly up through the Taurus Range to Antioch, the leading city in the district of Pisidia. It is significant that relatives of Sergius Paulus were prominent landowners in Pisidia, as local inscriptions indicate. Had the proconsul of Cyprus provided Paul with letters of introduction in Antioch in Pisidia, which was a Roman colony?

The book of Acts narrates Paul's visit to Antioch, including a lengthy account of his preaching in the synagogue. There was significant response to the missionaries in Antioch, including from gentiles in the city and in the whole region.

Forced out by local Jewish opposition, the two men travelled on from Antioch via a network of Roman roads to Iconium and Lystra where they typically met with fierce and painful opposition. After reaching Derbe, a minor settlement, they retraced their steps, encouraging the new churches as they went before eventually returning from Attalia to Antioch.

The entire round trip probably took between six to twelve months.

Crisis in Antioch (AD 48)

Paul and Barnabas returned to Antioch to find that Peter had now come to the Syrian capital. Although historically the founder and head of the mission to the Jews in Israel, Peter had come under increasing pressure from more nationalistic Jews in Jerusalem. Peter had laid hands of prayer on the unclean and heretical Samaritans and, more recently, had baptized a gentile family in Caesarea. More recently still, Peter had supported Paul against the demands to circumcise the gentile Titus in Jerusalem, after which he had in principle endorsed Paul's new circumcision-free mission to the gentiles. Peter's influence in Jerusalem as well as within wider Israel was now finished. This helps explain why he left Jerusalem for the more "open" church in Antioch.

At first Peter fell in with the liberality in Syrian Antioch where Jews and gentiles sat at table as equals, including at the Lord's Supper. But then messengers sent by James from Jerusalem had come to Antioch who applied pressure on Peter, insisting that Jewish believers eat separately from their gentile brethren. This was the situation that greeted Paul and Barnabas on their return from missions in central Asia Minor.

For Paul, once the element of *compulsion* had been introduced it meant that the "truth of the gospel" was threatened.[20] This was happening in Galatia where circumcision was being *forced* on gentiles and now in Antioch where James' messengers were *forcing* gentiles to adopt Jewish dietary practices.[21] The grace of God and the sufficiency of Christ's sacrifice were non-negotiable realities underlying "the truth of the gospel."

The matter was furiously debated in Jerusalem some months later where Peter took Paul's part. The Council of Jerusalem did not require gentile males to be circumcised but it did call on the gentiles to respect Jewish dietary and other scruples.[22]

---

20. Gal 2:5, 14.
21. Gal 2:3, 14; 5:12.
22. Acts 15:7–11; 15:19–21.

The Aegean Provinces (AD 49–57)

Our knowledge of Paul in the three provinces around the Aegean Sea is well documented in his letters from the period (1 and 2 Thessalonians, 1 and 2 Corinthians, Colossians, Philemon, Ephesians, and Romans) and in the Acts of the Apostles 16–20.

We are also able to anchor his Aegean missions chronologically. Paul arrived in Corinth in AD 50, a datum established by the arrival in Corinth of Jews exiled from Rome by Claudius in 49,[23] which is further confirmed by proconsul L. Junius Gallio's appointment in Achaia in mid-51.[24]

Paul's later decision to depart from the region was probably influenced by the news of Claudius' death in October AD 54. Paul's plan to withdraw from the Aegean region to visit Rome is consistent with the date of the death of Claudius and the lapse of his ban of Jews in Rome. This points to Paul writing 1 Corinthians early in 55.

In other words, our capacity to document these years depends on details in Paul's letters and the Acts of the Apostles and by key dates in the Roman world under Claudius Caesar, that is, the dates of Gallio's arrival in Corinth in 51 and Claudius' death in late 54.

Paul in Corinth (AD 50–52)

In AD 49 after establishing a church in Philippi Paul and his companions "passed through" Amphipolis and Apollonia to Thessalonica, a verb often used in a military context. The road on which they travelled was the Egnatian Way, Rome's great military highway across northern Greece.

Paul must have known that this road would have taken him to Rome within a matter of weeks, by the Egnatian Way to Dyrrachium, by sea to Brundisium at the heel of Italy, finally by the Appian Way up to Rome.

Paul may have intended to do precisely that. However, in AD 49 Claudius issued a decree expelling Jews from Rome,[25] the news of which would have come to Paul's attention at the very time he was probably contemplating setting out on that journey. Thus, instead of striking westward along the Egnatian Way to Rome Paul went first to Thessalonica, then to Berea where he established churches.

---

23. Acts 18:1–2; Suetonius, *Claudius* 25.4;

24. Bruce, *Acts of the Apostles*, 395.

25. Suetonius, *Claudius* 25.4; Acts 18:2.

Paul's Story 2: His Second Thirty Years (AD 34–65)

Paul then travelled south for a brief visit to Athens and then on to Corinth, where he remained for nearly two years. From Corinth Paul wrote 1 and 2 Thessalonians during his first visit and Romans during his final visit.

Corinth's unique location on a narrow isthmus meant considerable north-south land traffic and east-west sea traffic, bringing many visitors to the city, making it an ideal missionary base for Paul. Athens' heyday as an intellectual center lay in the past, but "new" Corinth, which was now a Roman colony, was a thriving commercial boomtown and the fourth city in the empire.

Paul would also have seen Corinth as a convenient city from which to reach Rome, a journey of just a few weeks. In AD 41 Claudius had rescinded a decree forbidding Jews assembling for worship and Paul may have hoped that Caesar would also cancel his decree of AD 49, thus allowing Jews to come to Rome. Paul had long hoped to come to the world capital.[26]

Paul in Ephesus (AD 52–55)

Paul left Corinth in AD 51 and made a brief visit to Ephesus en route to Jerusalem. He then revisited Antioch and travelled westward through southern Galatia, making pastoral calls on the churches as he went. He completed this vast circuit in AD 52, finally arriving in Ephesus, the major city on the western Aegean.

Paul remained in Ephesus for about three years where after three months of teaching in the synagogue he moved to a schoolhouse where he gave daily lectures. Ephesus was a harbor city where the great highway to the east began, making it comparable with Corinth as a strategic mission base for Paul.

Paul faced many hardships in Ephesus. He wrote of being "in danger every hour," of having "fought with beasts" and having "many adversaries," and of suffering from a near-death experience through a citywide riot.[27]

It appears that the moment it was possible for Paul to go to Rome he immediately planned to do so. Claudius died in October 54 when Paul was in Ephesus. It seems that was the signal for Paul to withdraw from the Aegean region and head at last to Rome.

---

26. Rom 1:13; 15:22.
27. Acts 16:23; 17:9, 14; 18:12; 1 Cor 15:30, 32; 16:9; Acts 19:23—20:1; 2 Cor 1:9.

First, however, he must finalize the collection from his mission churches in the Roman provinces of Galatia, Macedonia, Achaia, and Asia, and take the proceeds to Jerusalem. Initially Paul planned a well-organized, systematic farewell of his churches. He would leave Ephesus, travel north to Troas, cross over to Macedonia, then travel south to Corinth, and from there depart by sea to Palestine. So much for Paul's plans!

The Collection

Back in AD 47 Paul sought the goodwill of James, Cephas, and John for his westward mission to the gentiles. These leaders pointed to the poverty of the church in Jerusalem and asked Paul for assistance from the mission churches he would establish. The background to this was that from the middle forties the believers in the holy city, like other Jews, were suffering from a protracted famine that was to last many years.

Surviving documents from the era point to a sharp spike in grain prices. Queen Helena, of the kingdom of Adiabene (in northern Mesopotamia), who was a convert to Judaism, sent famine relief to the Jews in Jerusalem. During Paul's missions in Galatia and in the Aegean provinces, Paul secured the support of his mission churches for a major relief venture. Paul proposed that delegates from the churches should accompany him on his final visit to Jerusalem. Each delegate brought money from his cluster of churches.

Paul's commitment to this major undertaking reveals two aspects of his character. On the one hand, it points to his integrity in honoring his earlier undertaking. This is thrown into sharp relief by the fact that numbers of members of the Jerusalem church had attempted to overturn his work, notably in Galatia and Corinth. On the other hand, it shows Paul to have been a man of practical compassion. He promised to remember the poor, and he did.

Issues in Corinth

The moral crisis in Corinth, involving a man in an incestuous relationship with his mother (or step-mother), was not resolved by Paul's 1 Corinthian letter. Paul made an unscheduled visit to Corinth that proved "painful." The church was left divided with the matter unresolved. Paul sent Titus with a stern letter to sort things out.[28]

Soon afterwards the citywide riot broke out in Ephesus against Paul who was forced to flee for his life. He travelled north to Troas where he had planned to meet Titus and where he hoped against hope for good news from Corinth. Days passed and Paul became deeply anxious at the non-appearance of his trusted coworker.

The days were shortening, signalling the imminent end of shipboard travel during winter (October–February). So Paul travelled across to Neapolis in Macedonia expecting to find Titus there. Paul endured more anxiety from the non-appearance of his friend. Eventually Titus arrived bearing the good news that the incestuous man had repented, but also balancing bad news that Paul's reputation in Corinth was badly tarnished, and the even worse news of the arrival of a band of rival preachers from Jerusalem who were attempting to seize control of the church. Meanwhile the Corinthians had stopped contributing to the collection of money that was to be taken to Jerusalem.

These events threw Paul's plans for an orderly withdrawal into disarray. In Macedonia he halted his journey to Corinth. He must write yet another letter to this church, his passionate 2 Corinthians. Briefly, Paul wrote to rehabilitate his damaged reputation, inspire the Corinthians to resume and complete the collection, and—not least—to discredit the newly arrived preachers, whom he described as "peddlers" of the word, "super-apostles," and "false apostles."

Titus and others brought the letter to Corinth and Paul followed some weeks later, accompanied by Timothy and some Macedonian helpers.

From all accounts his third and final visit to Corinth proved successful. The Corinthians completed the collection and the rival preachers seemed to have returned, defeated, to Jerusalem. During his three-month sojourn in Corinth he wrote to the Roman Christians in his mission network to prepare them for his upcoming visit.

Summary of Paul's Aegean Ministry

Thanks to the book of Acts and the letters of Paul we are well placed to work out a chronology of Paul's missions in the provinces around the Aegean.

---

28. 2 Cor 2:3–4; 2:13.

	Letters from	Letters to
50–52	Corinth	1 and 2 Thessalonians
55	Ephesus	1 Corinthians, Colossians, Philemon, Ephesians
56/57	Berea (?)	2 Corinthians
57	Corinth	Romans

As we have noticed, Paul established churches in strategic locations, guided by a concern to touch the lives of passing travellers. In Macedonia he founded churches in Philippi and Thessalonica, cities located on the Egnatian Way, a highway that was thronged with travellers. Corinth, Ephesus, and Troas were port cities through which major roads passed (Corinth) or terminated (Ephesus, Troas). From Corinth the message of the gospel spread into "the whole of Achaia"[29] and from the lecture hall in Ephesus "all the residents of Asia heard the word of the Lord."[30]

We know of churches in Philippi, Thessalonica, Berea, Corinth, Ephesus, Colossae, Hierapolis, and Troas but there would have been many more that spread out from these nodal centers. Writing from Macedonia in 56, Paul refers to "the daily pressure on me of my anxiety for all the churches."[31] His words, "daily" pressure and "all the churches" suggest a considerable network of mission congregations in the Aegean provinces, and beyond.

Paul's years in the Aegean region (AD 50–57) represented his most significant mission. He brought the Christian message from the east to the west, to the most critical region of the civilized world, one moreover that was close to Rome. It was the region where most of his letters were written, including those that have proved his most influential.

Ironically, the region of his greatest achievement was the place where he lost his freedom. After leaving Corinth for Jerusalem in AD 57 Paul was imprisoned, first in Caesarea and then in Rome. Paul was a prisoner until his death in AD 65, apart from a brief period of freedom.

Paul in Palestine (AD 57–59)

Eventually in AD 57, he set out for Jerusalem with the money, hoping then to proceed directly to Rome. In this he was disappointed. He was imprisoned in Caesarea for about three years during which the Roman authorities

---

29. 2 Cor 1:1.
30. Acts 19:10.
31. 2 Cor 11:28.

Paul's Story 2: His Second Thirty Years (AD 34-65)

failed to resolve the accusations against him so that eventually he appealed as a Roman citizen for his case to be heard in Rome. The Roman authorities then escorted him by ship to Rome for trial by Nero Caesar.

Luke became Paul's companion AD 57-62 so that he was an eyewitness to most of the events he described in Acts 21-28. We know this because Luke wrote those chapters using the pronouns "we" and "us" to indicate to the readers that he was part of the narratives during those years.

Paul in Rome (AD 60-65)

Paul had often planned to come to Rome to lay an apostolic foundation for the faith in the world's capital.[32] He wrote of having been "prevented" and "hindered" from doing so, but does not say by whom. Almost certainly the problem was that Claudius Caesar had expelled the Jews from Rome in AD 49, effectively preventing Paul coming to Rome.

Paul's mission around the Aegean provinces AD 49-57 was a Plan B, until the way would be clear to make the westerly journey to Rome. News of the death of Claudius in late AD 54 was the signal for Paul to begin to withdraw from the three Roman provinces encircling the Aegean and to make his way to the world capital via Palestine.

Paul eventually arrived in Rome, but unexpectedly, as a prisoner who as a Roman citizen had appealed to Caesar to judge his case. Unfortunately, the book of Acts, which was so informative about missions in Galatia, Macedonia, Achaia, and Asia tells us little about Paul in Rome.

From the book of Acts we learn that Paul was placed under "open" arrest, with a soldier guarding him,[33] and that "he lived there two whole years at his own expense . . . welcoming all who came to him proclaiming the kingdom of God and teaching about the Lord Jesus Christ."[34] Those "two whole years" were between 60 and 62.

Paul wrote to the Philippians soon after this two-year period. By then he had been relocated in the precincts of the Praetorian Guard, the Caesar's bodyguard. In this new location he had made contact with "those of Caesar's household," which suggests that he had influenced attendants in the imperial household, perhaps even members of Nero's family.[35] Previously,

---

32. Rom 15:20-21; 1:13.
33. Acts 28:16.
34. Acts 28:30-31.
35. Phil 1:13; 4:22.

Paul had waited for two years for the trial process to begin, but his words in Philippians—"in my imprisonment and in the defense and confirmation of the gospel"[36]—imply that the trial had at last begun.

Paul's letter to the Philippians is cautiously confident of his release, enabling him to visit his friends in Macedonia.[37] But why was Paul confident of his release and his return to Philippi?

To answer this, we need to be reminded about the politics of Rome in the sixties. Nero Caesar was immature (a mere 25 in AD 62), preoccupied (with acting), and distracted (he had recently murdered his mother, Agrippina). Effectively Sextus Afranius Burrus (the Praetorian prefect), and Lucius Annaeus Seneca (Nero's speech-writer and chief advisor)[38] were administering Rome and its empire.

Almost certainly Paul's "appeal to Caesar," whose outcome he was awaiting as he was writing Philippians, would have been heard by Burrus and Seneca, rather than by Nero.

Seneca would have played a key role in a favorable decision for Paul. This is because Seneca's brother was the Gallio who had passed a good verdict on Paul in Corinth a decade earlier.[39] The Jews had charged Paul with creating an illegal assembly. (The only place of meeting the Romans permitted was a synagogue). Gallio, the proconsul of Achaia, had determined back then that Paul had not acted against Roman custom in establishing his meeting in Corinth. Paul's group, which was located next door to the synagogue, was merely another synagogue that Crispus the synagogue president was now attending. After serving his year-long appointment in Achaia Gallio returned to Rome where later he became consul in AD 55 (?). Seneca was consul in AD 56.

There can be little doubt that Gallio would have discussed Paul's case in Corinth with his brother Seneca. Thus, so far as Gallio was concerned, a precedent had been set. Paul was not guilty of any breach of Roman law.

---

36. Phil 1:7.

37. Phil 1:25–26.

38. For reference to Gallio (Novatus), Seneca's elder brother, see Wilson, *Seneca*, 251 (and index).

39. Acts 18:12–16. Gallio rejected the Jews' argument that Paul's meeting was a *concilium illicitum*. Crispus the president of the synagogue was now part of the new meeting, along with other Jews, including Paul; this was another synagogue. Gallio reasoned that "questions about words and names and your own (Jewish) law" should be sorted out within the Jewish community.

Paul's Story 2: His Second Thirty Years (AD 34–65)

This may have prompted Seneca's friend and colleague Burrus to release Paul.[40]

After AD 62 everything changed when Burrus died and was replaced by Tigellinus. From that time the tide was running against Seneca who attempted to retire from public life in AD 62. Three years later, Nero forced him to commit suicide.

Providentially for Paul, Burrus and Seneca were the men of influence during Paul's early years in Rome and made his release possible. After AD 62, however, Paul's protectors Burrus and Seneca were gone from the seat of influence.

Paul's Release

Paul's "pastoral" letters, Titus, 1 Timothy, and 2 Timothy imply that Paul was released from Rome and travelled back to the Aegean region.

From those letters we can piece together Paul's movements between his release (in ca. AD 62) and his death (in ca. AD 65). It is not possible to work out the precise sequence.

In Crete	Titus 1:5
In Macedonia: Nicopolis	Titus 3:12; 1 Tim 1:3; 3:14
In Asia: Troas, [Ephesus] and Miletus	2 Tim 4:13, 20
In Rome awaiting death	2 Tim 1:16–17; 4:6–7

Paul was under open arrest AD 60–62, freed to return to the Aegean region in 63/64 and then rearrested, brought back to Rome, and executed some time later.

Paul spent about five years in Rome (AD 60–65), including a period when he was absent (back in the Aegean region). It was an important period in Paul's ministry. He did, however, have a period of freedom shortly before his death in 65, when he returned briefly to the Aegean region.

---

40. Acts 28:16, 30; Phil 1:13; 4:22.

The Death of Paul

There is no direct account of Paul's death. It is to be inferred from the words of a church leader in Rome named Clement who wrote to the church in Corinth ca. 95.

> Let us set before us the noble examples who belong to our generation. Through resentment and envy the greatest and most righteous pillars of the Church were persecuted, and contended unto death. Let us set before our eyes the good apostles Peter ... and Paul.[41]

Clement's words may be deliberately vague because of possible further attacks on Christians. The emperor Domitian (AD 81–96), in whose era Clement wrote, was a known persecutor of Christians.

It is generally believed that Nero was responsible for the deaths of Peter and Paul. Nero made the Christians the scapegoats for the fire that destroyed three quarters of Rome in AD 64.[42]

The fire began July 19, so Nero's attack on the Christians probably occurred later that year. According to Tacitus they were killed by being torn apart by dogs or by crucifixion. It is possible that Paul the Roman citizen was not crucified but beheaded, perhaps some months later.

Based on early tradition and archaeology there is good reason to believe that Paul was buried outside the Aurelian walls, along the Ostian Way. The likely site of Paul's burial is preserved in the church known as "St. Paul outside the Walls."[43]

Reflection

By our estimate Paul was only sixty years old at the time of his death, being born in ca. AD 4. If our calculations are correct that the heavenly Jesus confronted Paul in ca. AD 34, it means he had been his servant for only thirty years. When we consider that Paul spent ten of those years in prison it makes his achievements all the more remarkable.

In the twenty-three years between AD 34 (his conversion) and AD 57 (his final return to Jerusalem) Paul planted the seeds of Christianity in a

---

41. 1 Clem 5.1–5 quoted in Bockmuehl, *Simon Peter in Scripture*, 109.
42. See Tacitus, *Annals of Imperial Rome* xv. 44.
43. See further Bruce, *Paul*, 450–51.

vast arc from Arabia to Greece. From those seeds Christian churches grew and flourished and in time developed into the Christendom of the Eastern Roman Empire based on Constantinople.

Beyond that, Paul's letters that addressed the Jewish-Christian counter-missionaries' attempt to impose "works of the law" on gentiles proved to be the basis for the Reformers' attack on the works-based religion of the medieval church. Their grasp of the noble notion of the grace of God owes much to Paul's arguments against Jewish-Christian legalism. Furthermore, Paul's insight into the others-centered life and death of Jesus gave shape to Paul's ethics that in turn have profoundly influenced western societies' norms of behavior. As noted, Paul was arguably the greatest thinker of the classical world whose legacy outstrips any of his contemporaries.

But it would not be true to the facts to portray Paul merely as a polemicist against legalism, or for that matter, as we shall see, against libertinism or elitism. We need to keep returning to Paul's "heart," his emotional attachment to Jesus whom he served. Paul served Jesus out of his love for him and this was in response to his Lord's love for Paul that was shown in Jesus' sacrificial death for him.

Five

Paul's Message: God's Son

It is critically important to identify the message that Paul brought to the people of the eastern Mediterranean. Fortunately, we are able to do this because Paul frequently echoes his primary message in the course of writing to his churches.

God's Call: Proclaim My Son

The place to begin is Paul's account of his initial "call" at Damascus, AD 34.

> [God] who called me by his grace, was pleased to reveal his Son to me, in order that I might preach him among the gentiles.[1]

Paul actually wrote that God revealed his Son *in*[2] Paul. More important even than the light Paul saw and the voice he heard was the inner light that God shone within him, the light that remained for the duration of his life.

> God has shone *in* our hearts to give the light of the knowledge of the glory of God in the face of Jesus Christ.[3]

Paul's words witness an astonishing transformation. He left Jerusalem with the darkened heart of the zealot seeking to punish the followers of the Nazarene. He arrived in Damascus with a heart suffused with light and

---

1. Gal 1:15–16.
2. Greek: *en* = "in."
3. 2 Cor 4:5.

Paul's Message: God's Son

love. What happened at Damascus was God's *conversion* of Paul and God's *call* to proclaim his Son among the gentiles. Conversion and call were two sides of the one God-given event.

God's *Son* was the message Paul was called to proclaim among the gentiles, that is, *throughout* the known world. Here it is of supreme importance to note the words, "his Son," that is, *God's* Son, indicating the unique filial relationship of Son to Father. Twice in his Letter to the Romans Paul refers to God's "*own* Son" driving home the Son-to-Father relationship between Jesus and God.[4] This is at one with Jesus' revelation of himself in the Gospels as *the* Son.[5]

Thus, Paul's message was focused on "the gospel of [God's] Son."[6] He reminded the Corinthian believers of the message on which the church was founded: "the Son of God whom we proclaimed among you, Silvanus, Timothy and I."[7]

Among the Gentiles

From the Damascus moment on Paul faithfully and effectively proclaimed God's Son to Jews and gentiles—to Jews in Damascus and to the gentile Arabs in Nabataea. On his return to native Syria and Cilicia in ca. AD 37 the reports of his fervent preaching of "the faith" reached distant Judea.[8] His labors for eight or so years in the province issued in the formation of gentile churches,[9] though details are lacking.

Paul established the church in Thessalonica in ca. AD 50. Shortly afterward he wrote from Corinth reminding these former idolaters of their response to the gospel.

> You turned to God from idols to serve the living and true God, and to wait for *his Son* from heaven, whom he raised from the dead, Jesus who delivers us from the wrath to come.[10]

---

4. Rom 8:3, 32.

5. For example, Mark 13:32; Matt 11:27 and parallels; as well as frequently in the Gospel of John.

6. Rom 1:9.

7. 2 Cor 1:19; also 1 Cor 3:11.

8. Gal 1:23; cf. 2:2.

9. Acts 15:23, 41.

10. 1 Thess 1:9–10.

For God has not destined us for wrath, but to obtain salvation through our Lord Jesus Christ, *who died for us*.[11]

These few words summarize the gospel that Paul had brought to them:

- You turned from idol-worship to serve the living and true God.
- You await the return from heaven of God's Son who died for you to deliver them from the coming wrathful judgment whom this God raised from the dead.

The Thessalonians' positive response to Paul's message indicates his initial, careful, point-by-point instruction about God and "his Son."

Paul, a Light to the Nations

Soon after Jesus' historic lifespan, Paul the persecutor became a disciple. He was no ordinary believer, however, but one who was convinced God had called him to become apostle to the gentiles. Paul devoted the remaining years of his life to this calling.

He was deeply aware of the *Servant Poems* in Isa 40–55, which foretold a servant of God bringing his light to the gentiles.

> I will give you [my servant] as a *light* to the nations that my salvation may reach to the ends of the earth.[12]

Paul came to understand that these words were to direct the course of his life. God had called him to bring the light of God to the world.

In Pisidian Antioch in ca. AD 48 Paul actually quoted Isa 49:6 to explain his mission to the unresponsive synagogue congregation.

> It was necessary that the word of God be spoken first to you [Jews]. Since you thrust it aside and judge yourselves unworthy of eternal life, behold, we are turning to the gentiles. For so the Lord has commanded us, saying, *I have made you a light for the gentiles, that you may bring salvation to the ends of the earth*.[13]

Paul was convinced that God had shone in his heart (at Damascus) so that, in turn, he was able to give that light to the people of the nations. Paul saw himself as "the light to the nations," though in a derived and dependent

---

11. 1 Thess 5:9–10.
12. Isa 49:6.
13. Acts 13:36–47.

sense since the true light to the nations was the servant, Jesus.[14] Paul established the pattern and practice of missionary vocation outside Israel. He was Jesus' missionary to the nations, fulfilling the prophecy of Isa 49:6.

Paul's Gospel to His Fellow-Jews: Rom 10

Romans 10 is a key text where we discover Paul's message to his fellow-Jews. It is clear from the opening verse that, as things stand, they are not saved ("My heart's desire and prayer to God for them is that they may be saved"— Rom 10:1). This is because they have not submitted to God's righteousness, which as he writes, is not found through the Law but only in Christ.

> Christ is the end of the law for righteousness to everyone who believes.[15]

A keyword here is "end" (*telos*), which means both the "goal" to which the Law pointed, but also its "termination." In other words, those under Law (i.e., the Jews) need to understand that Christ, not Law, is the pathway—the only pathway—to a right standing with God.

At the close of the chapter Paul observes that while the gentiles have heard and believed the message about Christ, his fellow-countrymen have heard the gospel but not believed it.

> Of Israel [Isaiah] says, "All day long I have held out my hands to a disobedient people.[16]

God's patience with his historic people in extending to them the message of Christ had been in vain. They are a "disobedient people."

The Old Covenant (i.e., the Law) Has "Ended": 2 Cor 3

In 2 Cor 3 Paul declares that the old covenant based on the "letter" (i.e., the Law) has now "ended." It had been written on "tablets of stone" (v. 3), was a "ministry of condemnation" (v. 9), and a "letter that kills" (v. 6). Paul stated that even during its currency, "it was being brought to an end (*telos*)" (v. 13).

---

14. Acts 13:47; 26:17, 23.
15. Rom 10:4.
16. Rom 10:21.

According to Paul the Law (or, "Moses" as shorthand) was only ever given to point beyond itself to its "end" or "goal," which was the coming of Christ. The old covenant was never permanent, but was given only to be abolished when Christ appeared.

This teaching answers the so-called "New Perspective"[17] on Paul, which states that even after the coming of Christ the Moses-covenant remained in place for the salvation of God's historic people, the Jews. It asserts that unless Jews deliberately opt out of that covenant it continues to apply.

According to this "perspective" gentiles find salvation through faith in Christ, but that Jews are already saved because the covenant remains and will remain current. Thus, there are two pathways to divine righteousness, one for Jews (Law), the other for gentiles (Christ).

This is not Paul's view, however. The response of faith in Christ, publicly confirmed in baptism, is the one and only way for Jews and gentiles to find the righteousness of God.

Israel Failed to Keep the Law

Paul makes it clear that Jews and gentiles, in fact all people, find God's gift of righteousness (justification) only through faith in the Son of God. Paul wrote the following words for his fellow-Jew, Peter.

> We ourselves are Jews by birth and not gentile sinners; yet we know that a person is not justified by works of the law but through faith in Jesus Christ, so we also have believed in Christ Jesus, in order to be justified by faith in Christ and not by works of the law, because by works of the law no one will be justified.[18]

Three times Paul stated that fellow-Jews like Peter and Paul are not justified by "works of the law" (male circumcision, dietary and purity rules, and observance of the calendar). Three times he states that "faith in Jesus Christ" is their route to divine justification.

The Faith of Abraham: Gal 3:6–14

Paul then establishes that the faith of Abraham and not the Law of Moses is the key to understanding the intent of the Scriptures.

17. See chapter 17.
18. Gal 2:15–16.

Paul's Message: God's Son

First, Paul directs the readers to the *faith* of Abraham.

> Abraham "*believed* God, and it was counted to him as righteousness." Know then that it is those of *faith* who are the sons of Abraham. And the Scripture, foreseeing that God would justify the gentiles by *faith*, preached the gospel beforehand to Abraham, saying, "In you shall all the nations be blessed." So then, those who are of *faith* are blessed along with Abraham, the man of *faith*.[19]

Of critical importance is v. 6 where Paul quotes Gen 15:6. God deemed or "reckoned" Abraham "righteous" on account of his trust in God's promise of a vast family of descendants. The whole of Rom 4 is Paul's exposition and application of Gen 15:6. That text opens the door to understanding the mind of Paul.

Next, however, he points to the impossibility of depending on law and "works of the law" for that right relationship with God.

> For all who rely on *works of the law* are under a curse; for it is written, "Cursed be everyone who does not abide by *all things written in the Book of the Law*, and do them." Now it is evident that no one is justified before God by *the law*, for "the righteous shall live by faith." But the *law* is not of faith, rather "the one who *does* them shall live by them." Christ redeemed us from the curse of the law by becoming a curse for us—for it is written, "Cursed is everyone who is hanged on a tree"—so that in Christ Jesus the blessing of Abraham might come to the gentiles, so that we might receive the promised Spirit through faith.[20]

Paul leaves us in no doubt that for Jews like himself and Peter the way of faith in Christ was the only way to acceptance with God. In short, then, it is clear that there are not two pathways to God, the law for Jews and faith for gentiles. Christ, and faith in Christ, is the one and only way.

In short, we can see how and why many Jews rejected Paul's message outright, in fact by an overwhelming majority.

Law versus faith, however, was not the only issue for Jews. How could the *man* Jesus be God's "own" Son when the daily creed declared, "Hear O Israel the Lord our God, the Lord is one"?[21] Furthermore, the same Scripture declared a man "hanged on a tree," as Jesus had been, to be "cursed by

---

19. Gal 3:6–9.
20. Gal 3:10–14.
21. Deut 6:4.

God."[22] A crucified man who was said to be the Son of God was difficult for Jews to accept.

The Olive Tree: Rom 11:13–24

What, then, about the covenant people to whom God had given his law? In Rom 9 Paul distinguishes between "the children of flesh" and "the children of promise." Only the children of promise are the true offspring of Abraham and the children of God.[23] In other words, the "true" Israel was not coextensive with the physical descendants of Abraham, even for those Jews who had been diligent in observing the Law of Moses.

Paul sums up his discussion of the future of Israel in his allegory of the olive tree. The tree has a "root," and that root was Christ. The main trunk of the tree represented the faith-based descendants of Abraham succeeded by those Jews who had responded by faith to Jesus the Christ. Some, however, have rejected him so that their branches have been removed from the trunk to make way for gentiles who have believed, who are now grafted into the tree.

This was and is a growing tree. In Paul's day it had at most a few thousand "branches," Jews and gentiles. Today, there are many millions who serve the "living and true God," dedicated by faith in his Son, crucified, risen, and returning.

Conclusion

God changed the man Paul, whom he had appointed to proclaim his Son. This Paul did in the hearing of Jews and gentiles throughout the remainder of his life. His message could be summed up in the name, Jesus Christ, God's Son and our Lord.

---

22. Deut 21:23.
23. Rom 9:7–9.

Six

The Example and Teaching of Jesus

PAUL WAS A MISSIONARY for Jesus, sacrificially devoted to serving him. His message was centered on Jesus, Messiah, Son of God, crucified but resurrected and returning.

For Paul's many critics, however, this is precisely the problem. Paul's message about Jesus, they say, was idiosyncratic, not at all the way Jesus himself would have framed it. Many follow William Wrede in saying it was Paul, not Jesus, who was the real founder of Christianity.

This, however, does not accord with the facts. The original disciples led by Peter after the first Easter quickly formulated their message about their crucified and risen master, buttressed by many prophetic texts that were now fulfilled in him. Luke records no less than five statements by Peter about Jesus as the Christ recorded in Acts 2–10. Two tightly formatted traditions quoted by Paul to the Corinthians in ca. AD 50, which were formulated very early in Jerusalem, exactly confirm the drift of Peter's speeches. Historically speaking, it was Peter who was the first theologian. Paul and others were deeply dependent on his primary shaping of the Christian faith.

Outside Damascus in ca. AD 34 God revealed his Son to Paul, and so changed his life's direction. To this "revelation" was added instruction about Jesus at Paul's baptism in the city, and most likely also from his new friends, the disciples in Damascus.

For the next three years the now-converted Paul told people in Damascus and Arabia about Jesus, the risen Son of God. Then he returned to Jerusalem and lodged with Peter for no less than fifteen days and also saw

James, the brother of Jesus.¹ Paul's engagement with Cephas, the leading disciple, and James, the brother of Jesus, provided the former Pharisee with extensive knowledge about Jesus, from his boyhood to his resurrection.

Contrary to his critics, Paul was not an eccentric loner who made up his own message. On the contrary, he was quite dependent on Peter and the Jerusalem Church for his detailed understanding about Jesus. However, unlike the Jerusalem Church Paul's missionary focus was on the non-Jews, the gentiles.

But their message about Jesus—the Jerusalem Church's and Paul's—was identical, as the three Jerusalem leaders agreed, and as he assured the Corinthian Church.²

In sum, then, Paul's radically changed thinking and life's direction took him deep inside the gentile world, but his message about Jesus was consistent with and dependent on the doctrines of the Jerusalem Church led by Peter.

Jesus as the Template for Christian Behavior

It is often remarked that Paul says little in his letters about the historical Jesus of Nazareth. True, we learn that Jesus came from a law-observant family, that he had a brother named James and a disciple named Cephas, that he had been crucified (i.e., by the Romans), and that he appeared alive to multiple witnesses. But Paul says nothing about Jesus' birthplace, his life story, or his miracles.

For some, these omissions prove that Paul was not interested in the human figure of Jesus, but only in the crucified and resurrected Redeemer. However, there is another explanation for Paul's silence. It is that Paul addressed these biographical details when he established the various churches. Reading Paul's letters suggests that the members of the churches were educated and thoughtful people who would have been curious to know about the Jesus whom Paul was proclaiming. Paul did not need to re-preach the details about Jesus of Nazareth in his letters since the members of the churches already knew them. Paul's letters addressed current pastoral matters.

---

1. Gal 1:18–19.
2. Gal 2:2; 1 Cor 15:11.

The Example and Teaching of Jesus

However, Paul did refer to the broad aspects of Jesus' life as setting examples of behavior for his followers. Consider the following passages.

His incarnation as example of generosity.

> For you know the grace of the Lord Jesus Christ, that though he was rich yet for your sake *he made himself poor* so that by his poverty you might become rich.[3]

His incarnation as example of humility.

> Have this mind among yourselves, which is yours in Christ Jesus, who, though he was in the form of God, did not count equality with God a thing to be grasped, but *emptied himself*, by *taking the form of a servant*, being born in the likeness of men. And being found in human form, he *humbled* himself by becoming obedient to the point of death, even death on a cross.[4]

His gentleness as the paradigm for Paul's ministry.

> I, Paul, myself entreat you, by the *meekness* and *gentleness* of Christ, I who am humble when face to face with you.[5]

His unselfish life was an example to "the strong" to accommodate "the weak."

> We who are strong ought to bear with the failings of the weak, and not to please ourselves; let each of us please his neighbor for his good, to edify him. For even the Christ did not *please* himself; but, as it is written, "The reproaches of those who reproached thee fell on me."[6]

His welcome of others as an example hospitality for the ethnically diverse.

> Welcome one another, therefore, as Christ has *welcomed* you, for the glory of God. For I tell you that Christ became a servant to the circumcised to show God's truthfulness, in order to confirm the promises given to the patriarchs, and in order that the gentiles might glorify God for his mercy.[7]

---

3. 2 Cor 8:9.
4. Phil 2:5–8.
5. 2 Cor 10:1.
6. Rom 15:1–3.
7. Rom 15:7–9.

His concern for salvation of others as the example to the Corinthians.

> Just as I try to please all men in everything I do, not seeking my own advantage, but that of many, that they may be saved. Be imitators of me, as I am of Christ.[8]

His sacrificial as love the example for believers.

> And walk in love, as Christ *loved* us and gave himself up for us, a fragrant offering and sacrifice to God.[9]

Paul reveals his knowledge of the historical Christ in the above passages. These touch on the broad outlines of the historical Christ—his lowering of himself in incarnation, his servant ministry, his loving and welcoming behavior, and his sacrificial death. Paul used these critical elements of the "story" of Christ's incarnation, ministry, and death as a template for his own life, and for the lives of believers in the churches of his mission. Each of the members were to model and shape their lives on Jesus.

Paul's Deference to the Words of Jesus

The major expanse of Paul's missionary years was between ca. AD 37–57 when he established congregations in Syria-Cilicia, Galatia, Macedonia, Achaia, and Asia. Paul may have written letters to the churches in Syria-Cilicia, but none have survived.

Between ca. AD 48–57, however, he wrote ten letters to the churches in the other four provinces.

When we study those letters closely we find echoes and quotations from the sources underlying the Gospels that would be incorporated later in those Gospels.

There is an observable pattern here. In the earliest letter (Galatians) there are just a few echoes of Jesus' words, but in the latest (Romans) there are many. This suggests that the "silos" containing the Gospel sources were being completed within that ten-year span. Where was this happening? Most probably these texts were being gathered and assembled in Jerusalem.

---

8. 1 Cor 10:33—11:1.
9. Eph 5:1.

The Example and Teaching of Jesus

(a) Galatians (ca. AD 48)

Galatians was Paul's earliest surviving letter, written from Antioch in ca. AD 48. Paul's reference to the law as "*yoke* of slavery" (5:1) appears to echo Jesus' words, "my *yoke* is easy, and my burden is light" (Matt 11:30). Because these words are found only in Matthew it means they belonged to a source known only to Matthew (commonly called "M").

(b) 1 Thessalonians

Paul wrote to the church in Thessalonica from Corinth in ca. AD 51. His reference to "the trumpet of God" (4:16) and the Lord's coming "like a thief in the night" echo Jesus' words in Matt 25:31 and 24:33 respectively (again, the "M" source).

(c) 1 Corinthians

Paul wrote 1 Corinthians from Ephesus in ca. AD 55 in which he cites three teachings of Jesus.

(i) On Marriage

> To the married I give this charge (not I, but the Lord): the wife should not separate from her husband . . . and the husband should not divorce his wife.[10]

Paul is loosely adapting several strands of Jesus' teaching:

> And he said to them, "Whoever divorces his wife and marries another commits adultery against her, and if she divorces her husband and marries another, she commits adultery."[11]

There is another point of contact. In 1 Cor 6:16 ("the two will become one flesh") Paul reflects Jesus' words in Mark 10:8 ("the two shall become one flesh. So they are no longer two but one flesh").

---

10. 1 Cor 7:10–11.
11. Mark 10:11.

The conclusion to be drawn is that Paul knew and understood Jesus' teaching on the permanence of marriage. Paul seems to be depending on an early Mark tradition.

(ii) Payment of Ministers

> In the same way, the Lord commanded that those who proclaim the gospel should get their living by the gospel.[12]

Paul is appealing to a teaching that "the Lord commanded." He is referring to Jesus' words quoted in nearly identical terms in Luke and Matthew.

> The laborer deserves his wages. (Luke 10:7)
> The laborer deserves his food. (Matt 10:10)

Matthew and Luke are quoting from a tradition to which both had access (commonly called "Q"). Both occur in Jesus' mission charges to his disciples. By the mid-fifties, if not earlier, Paul had access to this tradition.

(iii) The Lord's Supper Tradition

> For I received from the Lord what I also delivered to you, that the Lord Jesus on the night when he was betrayed took bread, and when he had given thanks, he broke it, and said, "This is my body which is for you. Do this in remembrance of me." In the same way also he took the cup, after supper, saying, "This cup is the new covenant in my blood. Do this, as often as you drink it, in remembrance of me."[13]

This is a liturgical tradition that Paul almost certainly received from Peter in Jerusalem in ca. AD 37 (Gal 1:18), and which he delivered to the Corinthians in ca. AD 50. We find these almost identical words in a Gospel-tradition.

> And he took bread, and when he had given thanks, he broke it and gave it to them, saying, "This is my body, which is given for you. Do this in remembrance of me." And likewise the cup after they

---

12. 1 Cor 9:14.
13. 1 Cor 11:23–25.

had eaten, saying, "This cup that is poured out for you is the new covenant in my blood."[14]

Luke 22:19–20 differs from the accounts of the Last Supper in Mark and Matthew, which suggests it belongs to a source only known to Luke (commonly called "L"). It is striking that it coincides almost exactly with the oral tradition that Paul quotes.

It appears that by the mid-fifties Paul had access to an earlier version of Mark, and the sources known as "Q" and "L."

(d) Romans

Paul wrote Romans in AD 57 during the three months (winter?) he spent in Corinth prior to his fateful return to Jerusalem (Acts 20:3). There are numerous references to, echoes from, and allusions to the teachings of Jesus in this letter.

(i) Romans 12

Rom 12:14	Bless those who persecute you; bless and do not curse them.
Luke 6:28a	Bless those who curse you, pray for those who abuse you.
Matt 5:44	Love your enemies, and pray for those who persecute you.

This is a "Q" source (loosely echoed).

Rom 12:17	Repay no one evil for evil, but give thought to do what is honorable in the sight of all.
Luke 6:29	To one who strikes you on the cheek, offer the other also, and from one who takes away your cloak do not withhold your tunic either.
Matt 5:39	But if anyone slaps you on the right cheek, turn to him the other also. And if anyone would sue you and take your tunic, let him have your cloak as well.

This is a "Q" source (loosely echoed).

---

14. Luke 22:19–20.

Rom 12:18   live peaceably with all.
Mark 9:50   be at peace with one another.
This is an early Mark source

Rom 12:20   if your enemy is hungry, feed him; if he is thirsty, give him something to drink. . . . Do not be overcome by evil, but overcome evil with good.
Luke 6:27   Love your enemies, do good to those who hate you.
Matt 5:44   Love your enemies and pray for those who persecute you.
This is a "Q" source.

Rom 13:7   Pay (Greek, *apodote*) to all what is owed to them.
Mark 12:17   Jesus said to them, "Render (Greek, *apodote*) to Caesar the things that are Caesar's."
This is an early Mark source.

Rom 14:14   I know and am persuaded in the Lord Jesus that nothing is unclean in itself.
Mark 7:15   There is nothing outside a person that by going into him can defile him.
This is an early Mark source.

Rom 14:20   Everything is indeed clean.
Mark 7:19   Thus [Jesus] declared all foods clean.
This is an early Mark source.

In Rom 12–14 Paul makes extensive references to the sources "Q" and (an early version of) Mark.

Summary

Analysis of Matthew and Luke identifies separate underlying sources—(early) Mark, "Q," "L," and "M." These were early texts based on Jesus' life story and his teaching, most probably compiled in Jerusalem. Eventually Matthew and Luke employed these sources in their finished Gospels.

How did Paul access these traditions? He visited Jerusalem in the years AD 37, 47, 49, and 52. Furthermore, he had extensive contact with

Jerusalem-based leaders—Barnabas in Antioch in ca. AD 46–48 and Cephas in Antioch in ca. AD 48.

The point to make to critics of Paul who say he departed from the teaching of Jesus is that his quotations of Jesus in his letters show that he deferred absolutely to the words of the one he called Lord.

Conclusion

The claim that Paul was a willful loner who devised his own version of Christianity does not bear careful scrutiny. While the Damascus "revelation" opened Paul's eyes to Jesus' identity as the Son of God, it is no less true that he depended on information about Jesus that had been pre-formulated in the Jerusalem church under the leadership of Peter. Immediately following the lifespan of Jesus, the disciples of Jesus, led by Peter, established the outline of their message and the traditions. Paul adapted and pastorally applied these doctrines to the churches he established.

While Paul is silent about biographical details concerning Jesus, presumably because the churches had already been informed about them, he does appeal to "broad brush" information about the one he served, for example, the humility of his incarnation and his others-centered self-sacrifice.

Furthermore, as details of Jesus' teaching became progressively available, so Paul increasingly applied those teachings to his churches. Paul submitted himself and his churches to those words of the Lord.

Seven

Paul's Vision: The Unification of Humanity

Paul's mission priority was "to the Jews first and also to the Greeks," which he implemented by going initially to the synagogue of a city. The learned visiting rabbi would explain how their Scriptures had been fulfilled by the Messiah Jesus. Those Jews who were thus persuaded would become informed foundation members of a newly established church. The apostle would then bring his message to the non-Jews in that city and those who responded would be connected to the Jewish believers in the newly formed congregation. The result, as envisaged and hoped for by Paul, was an ethnically mixed community of Jews and gentiles who shared a common faith in Christ Jesus, the Lord.

Paul saw himself as having a special mission to fulfill God's great promise to Abraham, that in him (that is, through a descendant) "all the families of the earth shall be blessed" (Gen 12:3). Paul saw this inclusion of the "families of the earth" occurring through a two-step process. He stated step one.

> Christ became a servant to the circumcised (the Jews) to show God's truthfulness, in order to confirm the promises given to the patriarchs, and in order that the gentiles might glorify God for his mercy.[1]

Christ "served" the Jews, as reported in the Gospels, as a stepping-stone to the gentiles, thus bringing to pass God's promises to the patriarchs, to Abraham in particular.

---

1. Rom 15:8–9.

Paul's Vision: The Unification of Humanity

Paul understood that he had a special role in the second step, God's outreach to the gentiles. He wrote that through him "Christ accomplished . . . the obedience of the gentiles" (Rom 15:19). Paul described himself as "an apostle to the gentiles" (Rom 11:13).

Sadly for Paul, the response of Jews to his message about their Messiah was progressively disappointing. He and others preached the gospel of Christ to the Jews in the synagogues but found them "a disobedient and contrary people" (Rom 10:21). This he explained as "a partial hardening" that "has come upon Israel" (Rom 11:25). As a result of the failure of the Jews to embrace the message, a "space" was provided for the inclusion of the gentiles.

Despite his disappointment about the current Jewish rejection of Christ, Paul was confident that his people, the Jews, would in fact embrace their Messiah later. The Lord's promises to Abraham still held true for his descendants despite the present "hardening." The consequence was that the church of the end time would be composed of believers who were Jews and believers who were gentiles (Rom 11:25–36). Then the Lord's vision to Abraham would become a reality.

This great hope Paul also expressed in Ephesians, a circular letter to a network of gentile churches not established by him:

> Therefore remember that at one time you gentiles in the flesh . . . were at that time separated from Christ, alienated from the commonwealth of Israel and strangers to the covenants of promise, having no hope and without God in the world. But now in Christ Jesus you who once were far off have been brought near by the blood of Christ.[2]

Paul saw this new humanity resulting from the reconciliation of individual Jews and individual gentiles through Christ to God, but also through Christ to one another.

> For he himself (Christ) is our peace, who has made us both one and has broken down in his flesh the dividing wall of hostility by abolishing the law of commandments expressed in ordinances, that he might create in himself one new man in place of the two, so making peace, and might reconcile us both to God in one body through the cross, thereby killing the hostility. And he came and preached peace to you who were far off and peace to those who were near.[3]

2. Eph 2:11–13.
3. Eph 2:14–17.

Evidence of this Jew-gentile unity was the sharing together of a common meal, including the Remembrance Meal established by Jesus at the Last Supper. Nothing exemplifies Paul's passion for this ethnic-religious unity more than his rejection of the attempt to separate the two groups at their meal together. The church in Antioch was a mixed church whose members happily ate together. But when conservative believers from Jerusalem sought to divide the meal time fellowship of the church in Antioch Paul saw it as an attempt to force the gentiles to convert to Judaism via male circumcision and other "works of the Law." Even Peter and Barnabas fell in with this attempt to proselytize the gentile believers. Paul, however, was adamant and effectively blocked this pressure to separate the gentile Christians from their Jewish brothers and sisters in Antioch (Gal 2:11–14).

Paul pointed out to Peter that he and Paul were both "sinners" who were "justified" only by their faith in the crucified and resurrected Christ (Gal 2:15–16). As Jewish believers, they were in no way superior to the gentiles who believed in Christ, and that, therefore, eating together was the right of both Jews and gentiles.

Paul made the same point in this famous statement:

> For in Christ Jesus you are all sons of God, through faith. For as many of you as were baptized into Christ have put on Christ. There is neither Jew nor Greek, there is neither slave nor free, there is no male and female, for you are all one in Christ Jesus. And if you are Christ's, then you are Abraham's offspring, heirs according to promise.[4]

The promise to Abraham was being realized in congregations of such remarkable racial, social, and gender diversity as founded by Paul.

The ancient world was interested in the unity of humanity. Alexander the Great was a philosopher as well as a military conqueror. His vision was to secure for all humanity "concord" (*homonoia*) to give to the nations peace and communion with one another.[5]

Alexander and his "successors" (his generals) conquered the eastern nations from Macedonia to India and established numerous Greek cities and the currency of the Greek language, institutions, and customs that would last for five centuries. But his dream of *homonoia* between the nations did not become a reality.

---

4. Gal 3:26–29.
5. See Barker, *From Alexander to Constantine*, 8.

Paul's Vision: The Unification of Humanity

Paul's vision was for Jews and gentiles to discover practical unity in these communities called churches. He travelled extensively preaching Christ to "the Jews first, but also to the Greeks." His long-term goal was the church of the end-time composed of Jews and gentiles (effectively humanity) drawn together by their common faith in the Messiah, Jesus.

We are now two millennia after Paul, yet his legacy continues in the millions of Christian congregations worldwide that follow his ideal of multiracial membership.

Eight

Paul's Traditions

A CAREFUL READING OF Paul's letters will identify numerous usages of the word "tradition."[1] We use the word for long-standing beliefs and practices as opposed to words like "contemporary" or "progressive."

In the Jewish world in Paul's day, however, tradition meant something quite different. A tradition was a body of teaching that a rabbi would deliver to a pupil to receive. Gamaliel, Paul's rabbi-teacher, would have delivered various traditions for his pupil to receive.

Paul chose to use this language for traditions that the leaders of Jerusalem Church had delivered for him to receive. He also employed this vocabulary for the traditions he had handed over to be received by the churches he had established. Some of these he delivered to the churches, having received them earlier in Jerusalem already pre-formulated. Others, he created himself.

Either way, these were items of teaching and ethical directions to follow for those who had been baptized as dedicated followers of the Lord Jesus Christ.

---

1. 1 Cor 11:2; Col 2:8; 2 Thess 2:14; 3:6. For "a teaching" see Rom 6:17; 16:17.

Paul's Traditions

Paul Delivered the Traditions: Theological and Liturgical

(a) The Easter Tradition

Writing in ca. AD 55 Paul reminded the Corinthian believers, "I delivered to you as of first importance what I also received."

He then rehearses the tradition he delivered to the church in ca. AD 50, which he had previously received, almost certainly from Peter in Jerusalem in ca. AD 37 when he returned from Damascus.[2] In brief, that tradition stated:

> Christ *died* for our sins, according to the scriptures. He was *buried*. He was *raised* on the third day, according to the scriptures. He *appeared* alive to many people, several of them named. Whether it was I or they [the other apostles] so we preach and so you [Corinthians] believed.[3]

(b) The Last Supper Tradition (Repeated in Full)

> For I received from the Lord what I also delivered to you, that the Lord Jesus on the night when he was betrayed took bread, and when he had given thanks, he broke it, and said, "This is my body which is for you. Do this in remembrance of me." In the same way also he took the cup, after supper, saying, "This cup is the new covenant in my blood. Do this, as often as you drink it, in remembrance of me."[4]

In ca. 37–53, Paul delivered these traditions he had received to the following churches:

37–46	In Syria-Cilicia
47–48	In Galatia
49	In Macedonia
50–52	In Achaia
53–56	In Asia

2. Gal 1:18.
3. 1 Cor 15:3–7, 11.
4. 1 Cor 11:23–25.

We are confident that the two quoted traditions that Paul delivered to the church in Corinth he also delivered to the other churches he had established. The Easter tradition and the Last Supper tradition would have been the doctrinal and liturgical bedrock for the churches founded by Paul, from Tarsus to Ephesus.

Supporting confirmation for Paul's practice as a traditor is found in his first letter to the Thessalonians that he wrote from Corinth to a church he had founded only a few months earlier:

> The word of the Lord sounded forth from you . . . how you turned to God from idols, to serve a living and true God and to wait for his Son from heaven whom he *raised from the dead*, Jesus who delivers us from the wrath to come.[5]

The responses of the Thessalonians corresponded to salient items in Paul's initial teaching—"turn away from idols to serve the true and living God" and "commit to the Son of God, his death, resurrection and return."

Paul Delivered the Traditions: Ethical

At the same time Paul also delivered ethics-based traditions to the churches. Our earliest source for the ethical traditions is his first letter to the Thessalonians. He begins the "ethical" section of the letter with these words:

> Finally, then, brothers, we ask and urge you in the Lord Jesus, that as you received from us how you ought to walk and to please God, just as you are doing, that you do so more and more. For you know what instructions we gave you through the Lord Jesus.[6]

In these few words we find the language of a rabbi delivering a body of teaching to a pupil: "you *received* . . . how you ought to *walk* . . . *instructions* we gave you."

First, he reinforces their obligation to control their sexual behavior, confining its expression to marriage. This was especially pertinent since idol worshippers, as these people had been, were also free and easy sexually. Idolatry and fornication were hand in glove; the worship of *many* gods was easily expressed in having *many* sexual partners. This instruction was not

---

5. 1 Thess 1:8–10.
6. 1 Thess 4:1–2.

only important for the individual but no less because adultery had a negative effect on the marriages of fellow-believers.

Paul reminds them, secondly, to "love one another" as they have been doing (not only in Thessalonica, but throughout the province) but to do so more and more. The whole life and ministry of Jesus is summed up in the word "love." By this word (Greek, *agapē*) Paul does not mean human friendship, family affection, or sexual love, but selfless, gracious care of other people.[7]

Thirdly, Paul taught them "to live quietly, and to mind your own affairs, and to work with your hands, as we instructed you, so that you may walk properly before outsiders and be dependent on no one." In short, he enjoined the work ethic so powerfully taught in the biblical wisdom literature (Proverbs especially).

Fourthly, later in the letter he refers negatively to drunkenness, a critical issue in those times.[8] Several things contributed to alcohol dependence. The absence of clean drinking water meant that people were forced to use wine instead. The socially popular drinking parties—the *Symposia*—which included drinking competitions, exposed the young and the old to the perils of alcohol.

As well, it was widely believed that a god (referred to as a *daemon*) spoke through the slurred speech of the drunkard. These and other factors exposed many people to the negative effects of alcohol.[9]

Other Traditions

Paul's letters imply other traditions that he delivered to the churches, even where that form of words is not used. One example is the "house table"

---

7. *Agapē* occurs infrequently in Greek literature and of uncertain meaning. But this word and its associates occur very frequently in the New Testament, overwhelmingly so in Paul's letters.

8. 1 Thess 5:7.

9. In the era of the New Testament, Pliny the Elder (*Natural History*, Book 14) described inebriation as unnatural but due entirely to natural causes that had nothing to do with inspiration by the gods. Pliny said that getting drunk "perverts men's minds and produces madness, having caused the commission of thousands of crimes" (14:137). According to Pliny, regular drinking shortened human life, and he wrote that "the crowning reward of drunkenness [is] monstrous licentiousness and delight in iniquity" (14.142). Pliny referred to the damage to society done by habitually drunk rulers like Mark Antony and Tiberius Caesar (14.146,148). He acknowledged the addictiveness of wine: "the habit of drinking increases the appetite for it" (14.147).

recorded in his letters to the Ephesians and the Colossians.[10] While Paul doesn't refer specifically to such instructions as traditions, it is likely that they were part of the body of teaching that he passed on to newly formed congregations.

Paul's direction for a wife to respect her husband in the Ephesian house table sets out the principle he applies in Corinth for her when prophesying, that is, culturally to acknowledge him as her "head."[11]

Paul frequently writes the words "we know" in his letters. He does this to remind the hearers of the letter about a tradition already received.

> *We know* that a person is not justified by works of the law but through faith in Jesus Christ, so we also have believed in Christ Jesus, in order to be justified by faith in Christ and not by works of the law, because by works of the law no one will be justified.[12]

> For *we know* that if the tent that is our earthly home is destroyed, we have a building from God, a house not made with hands, eternal in the heavens.[13]

> *We know* that Christ, being raised from the dead, will never die again; death no longer has dominion over him.[14]

It is evident, therefore, that Paul left the churches he established with extensive traditions related to key Christian doctrines and ethics. Paul commends the Corinthians because, as he wrote, "you hold to the *traditions* even as I *handed them over* to you." He is referring to the traditions about Easter and the Last Supper, as well as the ethical traditions.[15]

Believers are those who have "learned Christ," that is, who have heard and been taught and who are now walking according to Christ.[16] This is a

---

10. Echoes of such directions to wives, husbands, children, and slaves are also to be found in Jewish apologetic literature. Compare Josephus, *Against Apion* 2.190–219, a lengthy passage, with the brief statements in Eph 5:22–6:9; Col 3:18–4:1. Also (briefly), Philo, *Apology for the Jews* 7:14.

11. Eph 5:33; 1 Cor 11:5, 10.

12. Gal 2:16.

13. 2 Cor 5:1.

14. Rom 6:9.

15. 1 Cor 11:2; 11:23; 15:1–3.

16. Eph 4:20–21; 1:13; Col 2:6–7; 1 Thess 4:1; 2 Thess 3:15 ("So then, brothers, stand firm and hold to the traditions that you were taught by us, either by our spoken word, or by our letter.")

new way to live as received ultimately from Christ, handed over by Paul and received by believers in the churches.

Traditions in Paul's Network of Churches: Romans

In writing to his mission network in Rome in the final chapter of the letter, the apostle Paul was addressing dozens of people many of whom, but not all, had come under his ministry. Several times in his letter to the Romans he referred to *received* teaching.

> But thanks be to God, that you who were once slaves of sin have become obedient from the heart to the *standard* of teaching to which you were committed.[17]

The Greek word translated "standard" is *typos*, which means "fixed pattern." Since the beginning of chapter six is about the life-changing character of baptism, we should understand the standard of teaching to be a body of instruction that preceded baptism.

The delivering of a fixed body of teaching—as more fully revealed in 1 Corinthians and 1 Thessalonians—was fundamental to Paul's attitude to converts and to life within the churches.

Later in the Romans letter Paul warned his people to "watch out for those who cause divisions and create obstacles contrary to the doctrine (*didachē*) that you have been taught; avoid them."[18] These persons, whom he does not name, have opposed the traditions Paul delivered to his converts.

Evidently Paul expected the traditions he had formulated—theological and ethical—to be followed by the members in his network of churches.

The strictness by which Paul expected his traditions to be followed emerges from words later in that chapter. A wife who prophesied or prayed in the church meeting was to acknowledge her head, that is, their husband.

> If anyone is inclined to be contentious, we have no such practice, nor do the churches of God.[19]

Paul expected church members to know and follow the traditions he had delivered to the churches.

---

17. Rom 6:17.
18. Rom 16:17.
19. 1 Cor 11:16.

Extended Teaching

At the same time, however, there is more to Paul's letters than his reminders to the churches about foundational traditions that they have received. It was necessary sometimes to provide new teaching in response to questions or to departures from the traditions.

Paul usually (but not always) introduced important new exposition with the words, "I do not want you to be uninformed," for example, regarding the Holy Spirit and gifts in the church,[20] or the circumstances of believers who have died.[21]

Paul's churches faced many problems of which we become progressively more aware with the passage of time.

Paul's God-given genius was his capacity to extrapolate out from his traditions by lengthy instructions.

1 Cor 15:12–58	The resurrection of the dead
2 Cor 11:1—12:13	Paul's anti-triumphalist boasting

These examples were Paul's responses to various challenges, for example, Jewish Christian activists among the gentile Galatians, Greek antipathy to resurrection in Corinth, and triumphalist preachers in Corinth.

Whole tracts of Romans, Ephesians, and Colossians are extended teaching that is anchored in his tradition, teaching that he crafted in response to various theological challenges.

The Role of Tradition in the Letters of Paul

A major role of Paul's letters to the churches was to recall the members to the foundational traditions that were their bedrock. For example, he exhorts the Corinthians to flee from temple idolatry and from fornication, the Galatians to hold fast to faith in Christ alone, and the Philippians to strive for the unity of their church. As noted, Paul introduced new teaching in his letters, but he makes it clear that the churches must conform to the original traditions, theological and ethical.

---

20. 1 Cor 12:1.

21. 1 Cor 12:1; 1 Thess 4:13. Paul also uses this form of words in Greek in Rom 1:13; 11:25; 1 Cor 12:1.

Summary

Paul was a highly organized and meticulous teacher. His initial traditions that he delivered were theological (the Easter tradition—1 Cor 15:1–7), liturgical (the Last Supper tradition—1 Cor 11:23–25), and the ethical and relational traditions—e.g., 1 Thess 4:1–12.

Paul wrote to his churches to remind the members of the traditions, and to reinforce their message. Inevitably other issues arose, whether from the Jewish or the gentile quarter. Paul extends out from his core traditions with powerful and profound instructions for his churches. The care and weightiness of his letters implies that Paul did not expect them to be merely occasional, written just for the moment then put aside. Rather, it seems that Paul expected his letters to be canonical for his churches.

Nine

Paul's Mission Network

AT DAMASCUS GOD CALLED Paul to "proclaim his Son among the gentiles,"[1] that is, throughout the known world, but with particular concern for the non-Jews. Paul referred to this divine call as his "apostolic mission."[2] Peter had been given the apostolic mission to the Jews, and Paul had been given the apostolic mission to the gentiles. He explained it this way to the Galatian Christians:

> I had been entrusted with the gospel to the uncircumcised, just as Peter had been entrusted with the gospel to the circumcised (for he who worked through Peter for his *apostolic ministry* to the circumcised worked also through me for *mine* to the gentiles).[3]

Paul pursued this mission within its ethnic parameters from the time of the Damascus call in ca. AD 34. Fourteen years later at the meeting in Jerusalem the "pillar" apostles, James, Peter, and John, confirmed Paul's mission and message in the intervening years, in Damascus, Arabia, and Syria-Cilicia. Paul fulfilled this heavenly calling throughout the remainder of his life.

---

1. Gal 1:16.
2. Gal 2:8 (Greek, *apostolē*).
3. Gal 2:7–8.

Paul's Network of Churches

From the time Paul returned from Damascus via Jerusalem to his native Tarsus we see him establishing congregations.

(i) In Syria-Cilicia (AD 37–47)

The former persecutor's vigorous preaching in his home province came to the attention of the churches in Judea.[4] It is likely that much of this preaching occurred in the local synagogues, and equally likely that he received his five beatings for declaring that Christ crucified, not observance of the law, was the pathway to life.[5]

It is reasonable to assume that God-fearers in the synagogues were attracted to that circumcision-free message. Whatever the case, we know that by AD 49 Paul had created a network of gentile churches in his home province. The evidence for this is the letter from the Jerusalem Council in AD 49 directed "to the brothers who are of the *gentiles* in *Antioch* and *Syria* and *Cilicia*."[6]

(ii) The Galatian Churches (ca. AD 48)

After the meeting in Jerusalem in ca. AD 47, Paul and Barnabas returned to Antioch and soon afterward travelled to Cyprus, then to the coast of Pamphylia, and then up to the Roman cities of southern Galatia (Antioch in Pisidia, Iconium, Lystra, and Derbe) where they established the Galatian churches. These new congregations were predominantly composed of non-Jews. Later Paul addressed a letter to "the churches of Galatia," that is, to his mission network in that province.[7] Paul was to revisit these churches on at least two further occasions.[8]

---

4. Gal 1:21–23. For whatever reason Luke passes over Paul's years in Syria-Cilicia with few references, prompting these being called "the unknown years."

5. 2 Cor 11:24. Paul chose to endure this punishment instead of being excommunicated.

6. Acts 15:23, 41.

7. Gal 1:2.

8. Acts 16:1, 4–5; and 18:23.

Year		written from
48	Galatians	Antioch

(iii) The Churches in the Aegean Provinces (AD 50–57)

In ca. AD 49 Paul, with Silas and Timothy, travelled westward to the Aegean region. Over the next eight years with the help of newly appointed coworkers he established churches in Macedonia (Philippi, Thessalonica, Berea), Achaia (Corinth), and Asia (Ephesus, Colossae, Hierapolis). This was an exceptionally fruitful missionary period, as reflected in the numerous letters Paul wrote to the churches he had established.

Year		written from
50	1 Thessalonians	Corinth
51	2 Thessalonians	Corinth
	Ephesians	Ephesus[9]
	Colossians	Ephesus
	Philemon	Ephesus
55	1 Corinthians	Ephesus
56	2 Corinthians	Berea [?]

(iv) The Mission Network in Rome

Paul wrote to his mission network in Rome in the year ca. AD 57. He did not address the letter to the church in Rome (which was built on Peter, the "foundation" stone—Rom 15:20) but to the many people who belonged to a loose association of mission friends in their house-based meetings (Romans 16:3–16).

(v) Paul in Rome: His Supervision of the Churches

In ca. AD 60 Paul was transported to Rome as a prisoner attended by friends Luke and Aristarchus. Two years later he wrote from prison in Rome to the church in Philippi. In the course of the letter he addressed issues of disunity

---

9. These three closely connected "prison" epistles are best understood as having been written from Ephesus. Ephesus was a short distance from Colossae whereas Rome, the alternative provenance, is an impossibly far distance.

in Philippi while revealing an understanding of circumstances of fellow-believers in the Imperial capital.

During his brief time of freedom in ca. AD 63–64 Paul mentions a whole new group of colleagues in his first letter to Timothy and his letter to Titus. Re-arrested and repatriated to Rome for execution, he wrote a second letter to Timothy.

Paul's Mission Networks: "The Churches of the Gentiles"

From ca. AD 37 (his return to Tarsus) until ca. AD 65 (his death in Rome) Paul had been establishing and supervising networks of congregations. These are to be thought of as a Paul-led mission. As discussed earlier, there was a body of traditions that was the doctrinal basis for these churches, and a group of approved lieutenants who represented him in his absence.

Paul referred to his mission churches variously as "the churches of God," "all the churches," "the churches of the gentiles," and "the churches of Christ."[10]

Reflection

Paul's achievements (AD 37–57) are nothing short of amazing. In twenty years this travelling tradesman established and supervised congregations in five Roman provinces—Syria-Cilicia, Galatia, Macedonia, Achaia, and Asia. With a keen eye for strategic locations (ports, highway junctions) this Jewish man ensured that travellers had the opportunity to hear the good news about Jesus the Christ. As well, he established the practice of missionary outreach from these nodal bases for the formation of an ever-growing Christian movement.

This apostle recruited a body of skilled, loyal, and dedicated associates who continued his work even after his passing. The Pauline mission did not die with him, but continued.

Most importantly of all, Paul's traditions that he delivered to the churches soon became part of the canon of the New Testament. Paul's influence lived on through his letters, which were read in the churches.

By the beginning of the fourth century the political center of gravity had moved from Rome to Byzantium (renamed Constantinople). The

---

10. 2 Thess 1:4; 1 Cor 11:16; 7:17 cf. 4:17; Rom 16:4, 16.

Roman Empire in its eastern and Greek incarnation continued until the fall of Constantinople in AD 1453. The Byzantine Empire, which extended from the Balkans around the Levant to North Africa, was a Christian empire. But its foundations in the east were laid by the dedicated and gifted Paul of Tarsus, who was immediately followed by the apostle John, based in Ephesus.

Ten

Paul's Mission Coworkers

HOW CAN WE EXPLAIN Paul's achievements? Paul's letters reveal him to have been both highly intelligent and well educated. He writes in fluent Greek with a large vocabulary expressed in flawless grammar. His letters employ a wide variety of literary forms, including thanksgiving prayers, personal memoirs, ironic speeches, lyrical hymns, and carefully formatted teaching passages.

His expertise as a letter writer is consistent with what we know of Paul. He was born into a wealthy Jewish family who lived in the Roman province of Syria-Cilicia. His father was a Roman citizen and a citizen of his home city, Tarsus. The young Paul inherited both of these prized citizenships. His membership in a devout Jewish family exposed him to the teaching of the Greek translation of the Hebrew Scriptures, both at home, at the synagogue school and in the synagogue meetings.

The teenage Paul went to Jerusalem to study under the leading rabbi of the day, Gamaliel. Paul was a star pupil among the disciples of the great rabbi. Later, as a fully fledged Pharisee, Paul took the lead in the violent suppression of the new sect of Nazarenes. He was a highly focused and determined person, which helps explain his later achievements as a convert to Christ and as an apostle.

These elements in Paul—his intellect, his education, his "driven" temperament—were the qualities that marked the young man as suitable to go to Damascus to arrest the disciples who had fled there. When God converted Paul he also converted and enhanced his mind and re-directed his determination. From now on his passion was no longer the Law of Moses but the service of the Son of God. The astonished Christians in Judea said, "He who used to persecute us is now preaching the faith he once tried to destroy."[1]

Above all, it was God's conversion of Paul that explains his subsequent achievements and greatness. The now-converted Paul was highly motivated to connect people to Jesus and extremely hard working and innovative. He supported himself financially as a tent maker and underwent extreme privations in the pursuit of his ministry.[2]

He sustained the churches he had established by his pastoral letters, which addressed their current concerns. Often these letters were a church's only "scripture" to keep them on the right track theologically, spiritually, and ethically.

Paul's Coworkers

Something else that explains Paul's achievements was his capacity to recruit and retain workers for his mission. Paul established a large mission team of key people, who helped write his letters, then deliver and explain his letters, and carry forward the work on their own initiative.

This is well illustrated in Paul's connected letters to the church at Colossae and to Philemon, who led an adjunct church in the same city. Paul wrote both letters from Ephesus at the same time (in the middle fifties).

With Paul in Ephesus were Aristarchus, Mark (cousin of Barnabas), Jesus who was called Justus, Epaphras, Luke, and Demas. The bearer of the letters was Tychicus, accompanied by the returning runaway slave Onesimus. In Colossae were Archippus, Philemon, and Apphia, and in nearby Laodicea was Nympha, in whose house the church met.

Those two letters innocently show us that Paul had thirteen named associates in Ephesus and Colossae who were proactively committed to him and to his mission.

If we are looking for explanations for Paul's establishment of the new faith in the northeastern quadrant of the Roman Empire, we must include his astonishing capacity to multiply his own effectiveness through gifted and committed coworkers.

---

1. Gal 1:23.
2. 2 Cor 11:22—12:13.

Paul's List

To highlight Paul as a "team" man, we will list his known associates. The number would be expanded considerably if we included all twenty-six named persons who were to be greeted at the end of Romans.

There is a degree of fluidity in Paul's use of terms for his colleagues, whether "coworker" or "cosoldier." Some of those listed in Paul's letters may have offered hospitality, whereas others may have had more distinct leadership roles. However, the mere listing of the names serves to make the point: Paul was an effective team-builder and the success of his mission owes much to those who were his loyal colleagues.

- Journey from Antioch to Jerusalem (AD 47)
    Barnabas
    Titus
- Galatian mission (AD 48)
    Barnabas
    John Mark
- Aegean mission (AD 50–57)
    Silas (aka Silvanus)
    Timothy
    Luke
    Priscilla and Aquila
    Stephanas
    Titus
    Aristarchus
    Mark (cousin of Barnabas)
    Jesus who is called Justus
    Epaphras
    Demas
    Tychicus
    Archippus
    Philemon and Apphia
    Nympha
    Phoebe
    Lucius
    Jason
    Sosipater

Gaius
　　Erastus
- Mission in Rome (AD 57)
　　Priscilla and Aquila
　　Andronicus and Junia
- Mission in Philippi (AD 63)
　　Epaphroditus
　　Unnamed companion (Luke?)
- Mission in Crete (AD 63–64)
　　Titus
　　Zenas
　　Apollos
- Mission in Nicopolis, Macedonia (AD 63–64)
　　Artemas
　　Tychicus
- Mission in Ephesus and Asia (AD 65)
　　Timothy
　　Trophimus
　　Onesiphoros
　　Tychicus
- Mission in Troas (AD 65)
　　Carpus
- Galatia (AD 65)
　　Crescens
- Dalmatia (AD 65)
　　Titus
- Later mission in Rome (AD 65)
　　Onesiphorous
　　Eubulus
　　Pudens
　　Linus
　　Claudia
　　Artemas

We draw several conclusions from the (approximate) chronological listing of his associates.

Paul's Mission Coworkers

First, it is striking that Paul seems to have worked on his own in his early years as an apostle (AD 34–45). It was only when he began his westward thrust into the Roman world (to Cyprus and southern Galatia in AD 47) that we begin to notice his colleagues. The book of Acts refers to Paul's "disciples" in Damascus, but there are no names.[3] It is possible that he had recruited coworkers during his years in Syria-Cilicia, but no names are recorded, except perhaps Titus.

Second, his years in the Aegean provinces (Macedonia, Achaia, and Asia—AD 50–57) were marked by an astonishing build up of his mission team. Paul's associates appear to have contributed greatly to the spread of the gospel in that key area.

Third, as a prisoner facing death in Rome (in AD 65?) we notice that Paul's friends were scattered far and wide, in Crete, Asia, Achaia, Macedonia, and Dalmatia, as well as in Rome. Paul's work would continue after his death. We recall his words to Timothy: "What you have heard from me . . . entrust to faithful men who will be able to teach others also."[4]

This casts light on Paul's attitude to "the last days" about whose reality he firmly believed.[5] At the same time, however, he was providing for the ongoing and developing progress of the gospel message and the welfare of the churches. For Paul "the last days" and the ongoing mission were both realities, in no way contradictory.

Finally, Paul's team was not without its problems. Barnabas separated from Paul, though the two men remained in fellowship.[6] Barnabas' cousin, John Mark, had broken off from Paul during the Galatian mission, but was restored as a team member during the Aegean years.[7] Phygelus and Hermogenes and the believers in Asia "turned away" from Paul.[8] Demas "deserted" Paul and Alexander the coppersmith did him "much harm."[9] We need to be aware of setbacks and disappointments in Paul's ministry. Paul was no stranger to these.

We will now reflect on eight of Paul's key coworkers.

---

3. Acts 9:25.
4. 2 Tim 2:2.
5. 2 Tim 3:1.
6. 1 Cor 9:6.
7. Phil 24.
8. 2 Tim 1:15.
9. 2 Tim 4:10, 14.

1. Silvanus, Missionary and Translator

Silvanus was a Jew from Jerusalem but intriguingly had a Roman name, meaning "of the forest." Perhaps his parents or grandparents were originally from Italy but had migrated to Israel, either as free people or as slaves. In Paul's letters he is always "Silvanus" but in the book of Acts he is always "Silas," which was probably an abbreviation of Silvanus.

We first meet Silvanus in Jerusalem in AD 49 during the meeting of the apostles and elders that had been convened to resolve the issue of gentile believers observing Jewish religious practices. James, president of the meeting that included the whole church in Jerusalem, as well as the apostles and elders, concluded that gentiles who turned to God should not be troubled to adopt Jewish practices as a matter of necessity.

A letter was drafted to be sent to the church in Antioch where this had recently been an issue. The assembled church in Jerusalem wrote to the churches in Antioch, and in Syria-Cilicia "through the hands" of Silvanus and Judas Barsabbas (Acts 15:23). This means that Silvanus and his companion took the Aramaic words of the Jerusalem Church and translated them into Greek for the church in Antioch.

Many years later (in AD 64) Peter mentioned that he wrote his first letter "*through* Silvanus,"[10] suggesting that Silvanus had crafted Peter's Aramaic words and stilted Greek into the elegant Greek we find in this letter.

Acts 15:23 and 1 Pet 5:12 tell us that Silvanus was fluent in Aramaic and Greek, as well as most probably in Latin. Silvanus had several other important qualifications. Silvanus was a "prophet" and an effective encourager and teacher, and he was a Roman citizen.[11]

This was the man Paul chose as his senior companion instead of Barnabas for his next major missionary journey, which Paul may have hoped would take him all the way from Jerusalem to Rome.

Silvanus and Peter

Silvanus disappears from our records at that time, only to reappear a decade later in Rome. Since Peter visited Corinth in ca. AD 53 and then travelled to Rome, it is likely that Silvanus accompanied him and became a key part of the church in the world capital.

---

10. 1 Pet 5:12.
11. Acts 15:32; 16:37.

As noted, Peter mentions Silvanus in his first letter, in two matters. First, the linguistically gifted Silvanus was probably the scribe who interpreted Peter's words into the polished Greek of the letter. Secondly, Peter hints that he had authorized Silvanus to take the letter to the far-flung congregations in northern Asia Minor.[12]

This is the last we hear of this gifted man. Perhaps he died during this long and dangerous journey to Pontus, Galatia, Cappadocia Asia, and Bithynia. Or did he settle down somewhere and see out his days there? Or did he return to Rome and lose his life in Nero's mass slaughter of the Christians in AD 64?

2. Timothy, Paul's Leading Coworker

Paul would have met Timothy in AD 47 when he made his first visit to Lystra during the mission journey to the network of Roman cities in southern Galatia.

Timothy was the uncircumcised son of a Jewish mother and a gentile father. His name, Timothy, means "honoring to God" and reflects the monotheism of his mother rather than the polytheism of his gentile father. It seems that mother and son had become believers when Paul and Barnabas visited Lystra.

According to Luke, Timothy was "well spoken of by the brothers at Lystra and Iconium."[13] His reputation as a Christian was known even in the next city. The local elders in Lystra had "laid hands on" Timothy, recognizing in him "the gift of God."[14]

Timothy must have made a deep impression on Paul since he immediately recruited him to join Silvanus and to become the third member of Paul's mission team in their bold westward travels. This was in the year AD 49.

Timothy would have heard the reading of Paul's letter to the Galatians and noted the apostle's rejection of attempts to circumcise gentile men who had become believers. A mission team had come from Jerusalem that applied pressure on recent gentile converts to adopt Jewish practices like circumcision and the food laws.

---

12. 1 Pet 5:12.
13. Acts 16:2.
14. 1 Tim 4:14; 2 Tim 1:6.

It is surprising, therefore, that Paul circumcised Timothy before he set out with the apostle and Silvanus. It was widely known that Timothy's father was a "Greek" and that the young man was not circumcised. Because Paul usually preached first in the synagogues it was vital that his associates were circumcised Jews.

This young man was to become Paul's leading coworker and the chief lieutenant in Paul's mission team. Paul was later to say that he had "no one like him," and that he was "my beloved and faithful child in the Lord" and "my true child in the faith." Theirs was a father/son relationship.[15]

The Churches Around the Aegean

Thanks to Paul's letters that he wrote during his missions around the Aegean Sea (AD 50–57) we have a broad understanding of Timothy's movements.

49	In Macedonia	Acts 17:4; 1 Thess 3:2
50–52	In Corinth	Acts 18:5; 1 Thess 3:6: 2 Cor 11:9
52–54	In Ephesus	1 Cor 4:17; 16:10; Col 1:1; Phil 1:1
55–56	In Macedonia	Acts 19:22; 2 Cor 1:1
57	In Corinth	Rom 16:21
62	In Rome	Phil 1:1

During those years Timothy was coauthor with Paul of letters to the Thessalonians (AD 50–52, written from Corinth), to the Colossians and Philemon (AD 52–54, written from Ephesus), to the Corinthians (AD 56, written from Macedonia), and to the Philippians (AD 62, written from Rome).

Timothy was with Paul in Corinth in AD 57 at the time Paul wrote to the Romans.[16]

It is clear from his collaboration with Paul as a letter writer that Timothy was often by Paul's side. It is reasonable to think that because Paul specifically names him as coauthor of these letters that he contributed materially to the actual contents of the letters.

---

15. 1 Cor 4:17; 2 Tim 1:2; Phil 2:20; 1 Tim 1:2.
16. Rom 16:21.

At the same time, however, Timothy exercised ministry in Paul's absence.

50	Macedonia
52	Corinth
55	Corinth
56	Macedonia

Thus, whether Timothy was present or not with Paul he was a sure-footed, senior coworker in the Pauline mission.

Timothy and the Corinthians

Paul wrote 1 Corinthians in AD 56 at a time of tension and difficulty. The church in Corinth was torn between factional groups. Many were preoccupied with stylistic preaching instead of a simple Christ-centered message. Members were taking one another to the courts. Wealthy members were demeaning poorer members at the communion meal. Some were scoring points through their apparently superior speaking gifts. Others were questioning the resurrection, whether Christ's resurrection or their own future resurrection. Most serious of all was the church's failure to discipline a man who was sexually engaged with his mother (or step-mother).

When Paul wrote the letter he indicated that Timothy would visit them soon, the inference being that he would monitor their compliance with the instructions in the letter. Paul anticipated problems for Timothy, which is why he wrote this warning.

> When Timothy comes, see that you *put him at ease* among you, for he is doing the work of the Lord, as I am. So *let no one despise him*. Help him on his way *in peace*, that he may return to me.[17]

Despite Paul's request it seems that the Corinthians gave Timothy a rough time. Paul himself must then go to Corinth to sort out the problems. Paul referred to this as a "painful" visit, which reminds us how volatile things were in those times.

The Letter to the Hebrews

Timothy was also a trusted colleague of the anonymous author of Hebrews.

17. 1 Cor 16:10–11.

You should know that *our brother Timothy* has been released, with whom I shall see you if he comes soon.[18]

The author's reference to Timothy probably locates Hebrews to the period AD 50–64 when Timothy was active in the provinces around the Aegean Sea. This is the only reference to Timothy being in prison, but we assume it was in a major center like Corinth, Ephesus, or Philippi. This reference suggests that Timothy was a leader in his own right.

With Paul in Rome

In AD 57 Paul went to Jerusalem, accompanying the collection for the poor believers in the holy city. We lose sight of Timothy for about five years (AD 57–62). It is reasonable to think that he assumed leadership over the churches in the provinces that ringed the Aegean Sea. Perhaps in Paul's absence he travelled from church to church strengthening and encouraging the members.

Timothy reemerges in AD 62 in Rome as the coauthor of the Letter to the Philippians. Evidently the news of Paul's imprisonment in Rome had somehow reached Timothy. It was the measure of Timothy's devotion to his father-in-Christ that he travelled to Rome to be with him.

At the time Paul wrote to the Philippians he was facing trial from which, however, he expected to be found innocent and released. He hoped to travel to Philippi in the foreseeable future.[19] In the letter Paul planned to send Timothy ahead to Philippi.[20] Then Timothy travelled onwards from Philippi to Ephesus.[21]

Paul's Two Letters to Timothy (AD 63 and AD 65)

Paul was in Macedonia in AD 63 when he wrote his first letter to Timothy who was the leader of Paul's mission in Ephesus. Paul wrote aware of problems in the church in Ephesus that he calls on Timothy to confront. We may have thought these would have been due to persecution of Christians

---

18. Heb 13:23.
19. Phil 2:24.
20. Phil 2:19.
21. 1 Tim 1:3.

by hostile unbelievers. The difficulties, however, issued from the impact of false teachers within the Christian community.[22]

Paul wrote during the difficult time between the passing of the apostles and the formulation of official church doctrines a century later. Paul's instructions to Timothy were designed to carry the churches through this period of testing.

Nevertheless, Paul's first Letter to Timothy is not overburdened with these errors but also addresses other matters like the necessary qualities in "overseers" and deacons, good policies for the care of dependent widows, and the need to pay church leaders.

It was different with Paul's second letter to Timothy, which reflects a dramatic downturn in the situation in Ephesus. By then (AD 65) Paul was back in Rome, a prisoner in chains awaiting execution.[23] He grimly tells Timothy, "All who are in Asia have turned away from me,"[24] and refers to those times as "the last days."[25] There are now clear references to suffering arising from persecution.[26]

Paul's only close companion in his desperate last days was Luke.[27] He pleads with his younger friend to come to him before winter, bringing his cloak from Troas.[28] His reference to Troas suggests that Timothy will cross from there into Macedonia, follow the Egnatian Way to Dyrrachium on the west coast, and from there travel by sea to Brundisium, finally reaching Rome via the Appian Way. This would be an arduous journey of at least several months.

This is the last we hear of Timothy. Did he reach Rome before Paul's beheading? Nothing survives from those times to tell us. We assume Timothy took to heart Paul's two letters and made his own contribution to saving the apostolic faith in those difficult days.

---

22. 1 Tim 1:3–7; 4:1–5; 6:3–10.
23. 2 Tim 1:8, 17; 2:9; 4:6–8, 16–18.
24. 2 Tim 1:15.
25. 2 Tim 3:1.
26. 2 Tim 1:8–14; 2:8–13.
27. 2 Tim 4:11.
28. 2 Tim 4:13, 21.

Into the Future

Paul's two letters to Timothy address the worsening situation of the church in Ephesus and, indeed, in the wider province of Asia. Paul is not content, however, merely to buttress the churches against the challenges of the moment. He also makes provision for a good future of the faith.

> You then, my child, be strengthened by the grace that is in Christ Jesus, and what you have heard from me in the presence of many witnesses entrust to faithful men who will be able to teach others also.[29]

Paul's words, "*what* you have heard from me," refer to a body of key teaching about the Christian faith and the practicalities of the Christian life. Paul, having entrusted *this* to Timothy, directs him to deliver *it* to faithful men to teach in the present and coming generation.

Paul's plea was for Timothy to remain faithful to Jesus and the gospel message about him. No one knew better than Paul that the religious culture of the day would try to water down and restate that message and that Timothy would face ridicule and suffering as he defended "the faith once given to the saints" (to use the language of the Letter of Jude).

Paul's recruitment of a mission team appears to have begun in earnest from the time he set out westward in the year AD 49. Paul's decision not to include Barnabas and Mark in his team opened the way for Paul to invite first Silvanus, then Timothy to join him. Paul's apparent desire to press on to Rome was thwarted—it seems—by Claudius Caesar's exile of Jews from Rome in AD 49. This meant that Paul would concentrate for the moment on the many cities in the three provinces that ringed the Aegean.

During these seven or so years (AD 50–57) Paul established many churches in Macedonia, Achaia, and Asia, and recruited a growing band of workers for his mission. These men and women were Paul's envoys between himself and the churches and it is safe to say that they were a critical factor in the remarkable success of the Pauline mission to those provinces.

Paul recruited many colleagues during the years of his Aegean mission. Timothy, however, seems to have enjoyed a special place with Paul as a coauthor of letters, as Paul's envoy to the churches, and as a missionary minister in his own right. In writing to the Philippians in AD 62 Paul paid this supreme tribute to Timothy:

---

29. 2 Tim 2:1–2.

I have no one like him.... You know Timothy's proven worth, how as a son with a father he has served with me in the gospel.[30]

It would not be right to infer that it was merely a matter of "chemistry" that explained the depth of their relationship. A more fundamental explanation is to be found in their common commitment to and love of the Lord whom they served. Whether the two men were side-by-side or separate Paul was convinced that his friend was as committed, active, and hardworking as Paul himself had been.

3. Luke, Beloved Physician and Scholar

Like Silvanus and Timothy, Paul recruited Luke to his mission team during the critical period of his evangelism of the provinces that ringed the Aegean Sea. This happened in Troas, on the northwestern coast of the Aegean. We don't know when or why Luke came to be in Troas. Possibly Luke had come there as a missionary from Antioch.

Luke himself signals the occasion when he joined Paul's little band of associates. The anonymous author of Acts does this in the subtlest of ways, by changing the pronouns in the narrative of Acts from "they" to "we" to signal that *he* had become part of his own narrative, at least for several weeks. The first of the "we" passages in Acts begins in Troas and ends in Philippi. This occurred in AD 49.

Luke the Anonymous Author

Who was this anonymous author? Paul refers to "Luke" but he does not identify him as the author of Luke-Acts. But how could he? The author almost certainly wrote this *magnum opus* after the death of his friend, Paul.

Our only information, in fact, comes from the next century. Irenaeus, the most important church leader in the second century wrote, "Luke, the companion of Paul, put down in his book the gospel which Paul preached." Another source, the *Anti-Marcionite Prologue*, is also informative: "There is Luke, an Antiochene Syrian, a physician by profession, a disciple of the apostles."

---

30. Phil 2:20, 22.

Paul's References to Luke

There are only three specific references to Luke in the New Testament, each of them is found in the letters of Paul:

56	Luke my fellow-worker	Phil 24
56	Luke the beloved physician greets you	Col 4:14
65	Luke alone is with me	2 Tim 4:11

Luke's Greek name is *Loukas*. So is he one and the same person as the *Loukios* (Lucius) from Cyrene, one of the five leaders of the church in Antioch?[31] Because the spellings *Loukas* and *Loukios* were interchangeable, it is tempting to identify the two but we must be content to leave the question open.

What is clear from Paul's three references is first, that Luke, as his "fellow worker," was a senior colleague in the apostle's mission team; second, that he was a physician who was "beloved" by Paul; and finally that he alone in Rome stood by his friend who was facing execution in the near future.

Luke and Antioch

Many scholars believe that Luke was part of the church in Antioch. They base this belief in the many references to that metropolis in the Acts of the Apostles. The author knows a lot about this city and its church, suggesting that he had been a resident there.

Luke and Philippi

Luke spent about seven years in Philippi as a leader in the church. We know this because the first "we" passage begins with Paul, Silvanus, Timothy, and Luke crossing over from Troas to Philippi.[32] Immediately after Paul and his companions left Philippi the narrative reverts to "he . . . them." In AD 57, however, the narrative of the Acts returns to "we" and "us" when Paul passed through Philippi for the last time.[33] This suggests that Luke had remained in this city throughout the intervening period, AD 49–57.

---

31. Acts 13:1; also Rom 16:21.
32. Acts 16:10–12.
33. Acts 16:5–6.

There are several other clues that point to Luke being in Macedonia. In AD 56 Paul was in Macedonia where he wrote his Second Letter to the Corinthians. He mentions a delegation of Macedonian Christians who will be visiting Corinth, among them "the brother who is famous among all the churches for his preaching of the gospel. . . . He has been appointed by the churches to travel with us [with the collection of money back to Jerusalem]."[34] Who is this preacher who is so famous even in distant Corinth that Paul doesn't even need to give his name? Luke could have been that man.

Another clue is found in Paul's letter to the Philippians, which he wrote from Rome in AD 62. He addresses a significant member of the church as "true companion" [literally, "yokefellow"] to help these women [who were dividing the church]." This person, a close friend of Paul's, was so prominent that the Philippians knew his identity even though Paul doesn't name him. Once again this "true companion" could have been Luke.

Although we fall short of strong evidence that Paul was referring to Luke in his letters to the Corinthians and the Philippians it is quite likely that the apostle was referring to him. He was in Macedonia AD 49–57. Furthermore, Luke's majestic two-volume work identifies him as a person of exceptional ability. So, although we cannot prove the "famous preacher" from Macedonia or Paul's "true companion" from Philippi was Luke it is not clear who else would so neatly fulfill this high profile.

There is more that could be said about Luke based on his expansive writings. Enough has been written, however, to indicate that the "beloved physician" who was devoted to Paul was blessed with exceptional intellectual gifts. His contribution to the success of the Pauline missions is incalculable, a contribution that may have continued after the passing of the great apostle.

4. Priscilla and Aquila, Fellow Tent Makers

Paul first met this couple in Corinth in AD 50. Paul's preaching in Macedonia had provoked such a storm of opposition that he was forced to travel south, first to Athens and then to Corinth, capital of the Province of Achaia.

His first priority was to find the two fellow-Christians who were rumored to have arrived in Corinth from Rome. This couple were to become

---

34. 2 Cor 8:18–19.

among Paul's most trusted friends. Like Paul, they were tent makers, but more importantly Priscilla and Aquila were fellow Christians.

Some years later (in AD 57) Paul wrote this glowing reference to Priscilla and Aquila because they were exceptionally important in his mission network.

> Greet Prisca and Aquila, my fellow workers in Christ Jesus, who risked their necks for my life, to whom not only I give thanks but all the churches of the gentiles give thanks as well. Greet also the church in their house.[35]

Paul was incredibly thankful to them, but so too were all the churches of the gentiles.

How They Came to Be in Corinth

During the 40s there had been troubles in Rome within the Jewish community because of the preaching of Jesus the Christ in the synagogues. Priscilla and Aquila seem to have been leaders among the Jewish Christians and quite possibly were among those who contributed to the division among the wider community of Jews in Rome. We do not know how they became Christians.

Claudius Caesar, who was known to hate public disorder, took the drastic step of ordering all the Jews, Christian and non-Christian, from the city. This was in AD 49.

This was not the catastrophe to Priscilla and Aquila that it might have been to others expelled from Rome. This couple were not merely artisans who made and repaired tents and other leather items. They also were travelling merchants who purchased quantities of raw leather, from which they made tents, saddles, shoes, and other leather goods. Relocating from Rome to Corinth might not have been the problem to them it would have been to others.

Priscilla's Prominence

Of the six references to Priscilla and Aquila in the Acts of the Apostles and Paul's letters, her name precedes his on four occasions. Aquila was a Jew

---

35. Rom 16:3–5

but Priscilla may have been a gentile. Priscilla's formal name was Prisca. It is possible that she was related to a famous Roman family, the *gens Prisca*.

Whatever the reason was for the prior order of her name it is safe to conclude that she was socially and financially more prominent than Aquila.

The first century had become the era of the "new" Roman woman, based on the higher social prominence of aristocratic women like Livia, wife of Augustus. We think, for example, of Chloe in Corinth, Phoebe of Cenchreae, Lydia, Euodia, and Syntyche of Philippi. In the first century Roman women could own property in their own right and also initiate divorce. Christian women like these appear to have belonged to the new wave of socially advanced women in the Roman world of the first century.

Their Leadership

After Corinth (AD 50–52) we meet them next in Ephesus (AD 53–55), then in Rome (AD 56–?), and finally in Ephesus again (AD 64). Once Paul passes from history (AD 65) we lose sight of them. These movements suggest that they had business branches in several cities.

They were hosts of Paul in Corinth and Ephesus and most probably would have fulfilled that role also in Rome, had Paul reached the city as a free man. But leaders they surely were. A church met in their home in Ephesus and also in Rome.

Priscilla, Aquila, and Apollos

During their time in Ephesus a number of disciples of John the Baptist arrived, among them an Alexandrian named Apollos. We assume that these men were Jews who had been in Palestine in AD 28–29 when John the Baptist was having such a profound influence. Apollos was named after the god Apollo, which suggests that he had been converted from paganism to the Jewish faith.

John the Baptist preached that Jesus was the Messiah and no doubt would have taught more extensively about Jesus had his martyr's death not intervened. As a consequence, Apollos did not understand about the saving death of Jesus, his resurrection, and the blessings of the Holy Spirit to believers.

Apollos was a passionate preacher in the synagogue in Ephesus. When Priscilla and Aquila heard him, but noted that his understanding was incomplete, "they took him and explained the way of God more accurately." With the encouragement of the believers in Ephesus this man travelled across to Corinth where he preached powerfully and effectively in the synagogue.

Later, he returned to Ephesus where Paul subsequently referred to him as "our brother Apollos." At the same time, however, Apollos was on the edge of Paul's circle; he was not Paul's coworker. It is possible that the Alexandrian Jew Apollos was the anonymous author of the Letter to the Hebrews. Whether or not Apollos was that writer, he was a powerful preacher of the gospel message and for that we have to acknowledge the good influence of Priscilla and Aquila.

Priscilla and Aquila were among those who were closest to Paul, along with Titus, Timothy, and Luke. They were initiative taking leaders and loyal coworkers in Paul's great missionary enterprise. At the same time, however, we see them as leaders in their own right.

5. Philemon in Colossae

In AD 55, toward the end of Paul's Aegean mission, he wrote to a friend named Philemon appealing to him to receive back his runaway slave, Onesimus.

Paul's Letter to Philemon is a revelation of Paul's leadership in a far-reaching missionary network. Although Paul had not yet visited Colossae, his fellow-workers Epaphras, Philemon, and Archippus, represented him there. Paul sent greetings from Mark, Aristarchus, Demas, and Luke who were in Ephesus, along with "Jesus who is called Justus" whose name appears in Paul's companion Letter to the Colossians. Paul's success in recruiting this small army of mission-colleagues helps explain the success of Paul's evangelism and church-planting program.

This short epistle of only 335 words reveals Paul to have been an active evangelist but also a warm-hearted and caring pastor. His appeal to Philemon is based on grace and it seeks a merciful outcome for the runaway slave. Paul mentions no less than ten people by name, whether as "brother" or "sister," or "fellow-worker" or "fellow-prisoner."

6. Titus, the Diplomat

Titus in Antioch

The name Titus is Roman. We do not know if Titus had come from Rome to the east, or was the son of forbears who had settled there. Antioch was a major garrison city. There may have been military connections that brought Titus or members of his family to this city on the fringes of the Roman Empire.

Titus was a gentile apparently converted in Syria-Cilicia, whom Paul brought from Antioch to Jerusalem in AD 47. He was living evidence of Paul's effective missionary work among non-Jews. Titus was also an example of hoped-for mission success among the gentiles in future mission areas.

Conservative Jewish Christians in Jerusalem (whom Paul calls "false brothers") attempted to force the circumcision of Titus, but were not supported by the three "pillar" apostles, James, Cephas, and John.[36] The three leaders recognized Titus as a brother and joined hands in fellowship with Barnabas and Paul for their hoped-for further mission to the gentiles.

So far as we know Titus remained in Antioch after Paul had left for his major journey west in AD 49.

Titus in Ephesus

Paul returned briefly to Jerusalem and Antioch in ca. AD 52. It appears that Paul recruited Titus for ministry back to Ephesus. One of Titus's first tasks was to establish the relief-collection in Corinth.[37]

Not long afterward bad news from Corinth began to reach Paul. Of great concern was the news that a man was sexually engaged with his mother (or step-mother).[38] In response to these, Paul wrote 1 Corinthians (in early AD 55) and indicated that Timothy would come soon. Reading between the lines it seems that Timothy's mission was unsuccessful, making it necessary for Paul himself to visit Corinth, a visit that was also unsuccessful. Paul referred to it as "painful."[39]

---

36. Gal 2:1–9.
37. 2 Cor 8:6.
38. 1 Cor 5:1.
39. 2 Cor 2:1.

Paul then dispatched Titus with a "tearful" letter, which would be the basis for rescuing the situation in Corinth.[40]

It was arranged that Titus would report back to Paul in Troas, but he failed to arrive. Paul then crossed over to Macedonia where Titus eventually returned to Paul. Titus had brought Paul the good news of the offender's expulsion, although the now penitent man had not been restored to the church.[41] Titus had also brought the very bad news of the arrival of some rival preachers with a heretical message who were attempting to seize the church from Paul's leadership.[42] Part of the problem was that outwardly these newcomers were impressive wordsmiths, more so than Paul.

Titus in Macedonia

Titus's battery of news, good and bad, prompted Paul to write yet again to Corinth. This he did in Macedonia (probably Berea) and with the assistance of Timothy as coauthor.

Broadly speaking, 2 Corinthians addresses three major issues: Paul's explanation of why he wrote a letter instead of returning directly; their need to restore the now penitent offender; and his unmasking of the rival preachers whom he calls "peddlers of the word," "super-apostles," and "false apostles."[43]

Very importantly, Paul exhorted the Corinthians to complete the relief-collection, which had lapsed as a symptom of the break down of relationships with Paul. Their completion of the collection would send the message that they had heeded the message of this letter.

A problem for Paul was that some of the Corinthians questioned his integrity in money matters, perhaps even suspecting him of planning to steal the collection money. Paul strongly denies this but also points to the obvious honesty of Titus, his envoy. Just as Titus his colleague is honest, so too is Paul.[44]

Once again the task of delivering a letter fell to Titus, who was now to make his third visit to Corinth. The responsibility for reading and

---

40. 2 Cor 2:4.
41. 2 Cor 2:5–11.
42. 2 Cor 11:4–5.
43. 2 Cor 2:17; 11:5, 13; 12:11
44. 2 Cor 12:16–18.

explaining the letter would fall to him. This was no easy task since the letter is long, passionate, and at points confronting.

Yet the evidence points to the Corinthians having complied with the letter. They welcomed Paul when he arrived a few weeks later. For three months (probably winter when the shipping lanes were closed) he lodged with Gaius in whose home the whole church met.[45] The members completed the collection of money for fellow-believers in Judea. The church withdrew its welcome to the rival preachers. And, not least, they preserved and circulated the letter we know as 2 Corinthians, effectively securing its place in the canon of the New Testament.

Paul finished his strained relationships with the Corinthians on a high note and for this he was grateful to the Lord, but no less to the patience and wisdom of Titus. Titus must have been a truly remarkable man to win over this difficult and divided church.

Titus in Crete (AD 63/64)

After his release from prison in Rome Paul, in company with Titus, went to Crete to evangelize the people of the island. Paul then travelled to Nicopolis on the western coast of Greece where he planned to spend the winter.[46]

Paul directed Titus to come to him after he appointed "elders in every town"[47] and to provide a pattern of godly behavior for them and, indeed, for all the believers in Crete.

> As for you, teach what accords with sound doctrine. . . . Show yourself in all respects to be a model of good works, and in your teaching show integrity, dignity, and sound speech that cannot be condemned, so that an opponent may be put to shame, having nothing evil to say about us. . . . Declare these things; exhort and rebuke with all authority. Let no one disregard you.[48]

Paul devoted a whole letter instructing Titus and through him the Christians in Crete. It is not too much to say that Titus laid the foundation of Christianity on that island.

---

45. Rom 16:23; Acts 20:3.
46. Titus 3:12.
47. Titus 1:5.
48. Titus 2:1, 7–8, 15.

Titus in Dalmatia (AD 65)

In his final letter written shortly before his death Paul mentions the whereabouts of some of his key coworkers. Regarding Titus all Paul said was: "Titus [has gone] to Dalmatia,"[49] that is, the Roman province of that name.

The geography is important. If we travel north from Nicopolis along the Adriatic coastline we soon come to Dalmatia. It appears that when Titus came from Crete to Paul in Nicopolis it was not long before one or other of the two men thought it would be good to take the gospel message to the strategic region to the north.

Dalmatia became one of the most concentrated and populous Christian regions in the known world. So powerful was the Christian presence in the region that it provoked the Emperor Diocletian late in the third century to attempt to persecute it out of existence. Christianity survived and proved to the Romans that it was worthy basis on which to help the empire to survive. The Emperor Constantine, who converted the empire to Christianity, was from Serbia, close to the Dalmatian coast.

We may assume that Titus followed the same strategy in Dalmatia as in Crete. He preached the gospel, gathered believers into congregations, and appointed elders to provide pastoral care of the members.

We are able to trace the movements of Titus for about twenty years (AD 47–65). We are in the dark about his age, origins, education, and marital status. Our knowledge is restricted to his Roman name, gentile ethnicity, and the various places to which he travelled—Antioch, Jerusalem, Ephesus, Corinth, Crete, and Dalmatia. We know nothing before we meet him in Jerusalem (AD 47) and nothing afterward in Dalmatia (AD 65).

From the Jerusalem visit we conclude that Titus was a man of strong and clear Christian conviction. Our most extended glimpse of him is as one who visited Corinth as Paul's ambassador, to initiate the collection, to bring the stern "tearful" letter and, later, to deliver the hard-hitting 2 Corinthians. Titus emerges as a tactful and patient man who manages to win over the Corinthians in ways that Timothy and Paul failed to do. From his time in Crete we see Titus as an evangelist and supervising pastor who consolidated Christianity among the people of Crete. Finally, we see this man in Dalmatia where, we confidently assume, he faithfully preached the gospel and established worthy patterns of local church leadership.

---

49. 2 Tim 4:10.

Although our knowledge of Titus is limited, the little we have points to an admirable man whose gifts and temperament the Lord used in significant ways.

7. Phoebe, Patroness in Cenchreae

> I commend to you our sister Phoebe, a servant of the church at Cenchreae, that you may welcome her in the Lord in a way worthy of the saints, and help her in whatever she may need from you, for she has been a patron of many and of myself as well.[50]

Paul begins the final part of Romans with a formal commendation of Phoebe, whom he had appointed to deliver the letter to the apostle's mission network in Rome. Her journey of several weeks would have involved a sea voyage from Lechaion to Brundisium on the heel of Italy followed by an overland journey up the Appian Way. Once in Rome Phoebe would have sought a contact address, most likely the home of Priscilla and Aquila. We assume that Phoebe did not travel alone.

Once in Rome, Phoebe would have read the letter to the various gatherings of believers. Phoebe takes her place alongside other apostolic delegates privileged to carry the letters to the churches.[51]

Phoebe is one of a number of women in Paul's mission whose names are mentioned independently of a husband, for example, Chloe in Corinth, Lydia, Euodia, and Syntyche in Philippi and Mary in Rome. They may have been widows, but it is equally likely that they were socially and financially more prominent than their husbands.

Paul refers to Phoebe as a *prostatis*, which means "patroness" (or "benefactress") and points to her social and economic eminence. By the time Paul wrote this letter, Roman women had come to enjoy many privileges, including owning property in their own right, initiating divorce, and conducting a business (as Lydia did).

Such a woman was mentioned in Corinth only a few years before Paul came to the city.

---

50. Rom 16:1-2.

51. For example, Timothy and Titus to the Corinthians (1 Cor 4:17; 16:10; 2 Cor 8:16-18; 12:18); Tychicus to the Ephesian and Colossian congregations (Eph 6:21-22; Col 4:7-8); Epaphroditus to the Philippians (Phil 2:25-30); and Silvanus to the congregations in Asia Minor (1 Pet 5:12).

> Junia Theodora, a Roman resident in Corinth, a woman held in highest honor . . . who copiously supported from her own means many of our citizens with generosity . . . displaying her patronage (*prostasian*).[52]

Phoebe exercised her patronage and benefaction as a servant (*diakonos*) of the church in Cenchreae, a daughter church of Corinth. She had been "a patron of many and of myself," wrote Paul.

It is striking that the keywords about Phoebe in this passage are anticipated a few chapters earlier:

> Having gifts that differ according to the grace given to us . . . if service (*diakonia*), in our serving . . . if for helping (*proistameno*s [a verbal form of *prostatis*], with zeal.[53]

Taken together *prostatis* and *diakonia* indicate Phoebe's patronage was expressed functionally in active service of church members.

Phoebe's home was the meeting place of the congregation in Cenchreae. There she provided hospitality for the members but also lodgings for travelling missionaries, including Paul. Paul requested that the Romans minister to Phoebe in the very way she has "helped many" (including him).

Paul is unfairly called a misogynist yet the reality is that he accepted hospitality from Lydia, worked side by side in gospel ministry with Euodia and Syntyche, commended Mary for her hard work, and entrusted his manuscript of Romans to Phoebe for safe carriage to Rome and for clarification of its teaching.

8. Epaphroditus, the Carer[54]

Epaphroditus is a Greek name meaning "lovely, charming, amiable," and is derived from the name Aphrodite, the goddess of love. It is almost certain, therefore, that he was a gentile convert although it is possible that he had become a God-fearer (a gentile who attended the synagogue) prior to his Christian conversion. His name only appears in the New Testament in this letter.

There were several points of connection between Philippi and Rome. Philippi was a Roman colony, a miniature of the capital, where many retired

---

52. Lefkowitz and Fant, *Women's Life*, 207, 208.
53. Rom 12:7–8 (ESV adapted).
54. Phil 2:25–30; 4:18.

legionaries settled. Some of those veterans had previously belonged to the Rome-based Praetorian Guard, who currently had custody of Paul. A coin minted in Philippi from the time of Claudius (AD 51–54) or Nero (AD 54–68) bears the words COHOR(tes) PRAE(toriae) PHIL(ippensis), which means "Praetorian Cohorts of Philippi."

Perhaps Epaphroditus or other members of the Philippian church knew local retired Praetorians who could provide him with a letter of introduction or some other means of access to Paul's custodians in Rome.

Epaphroditus had made the long journey from Philippi to Rome. He fell ill either en route or on arrival. Given the physical demands of such a journey, the lack of clean drinking water, and the unhygienic nature of way houses and inns, it is no surprise that the Philippian envoy became so sick that he almost died.

No less that three times Paul refers to the dire state of Epaphroditus's health: "he was ill, near to death" (v. 27); "he nearly died" (v. 30); he "risked his life" (v. 31). Now he must make the long, perilous journey back to Philippi, probably as the bearer of this letter.

It is significant that Paul makes so much of Epaphroditus's illness. In that culture "loss of face" (shame) was extremely important. Epaphroditus probably felt ashamed that he had failed to fulfill the objective of his journey on behalf of the congregation in Philippi and perhaps dreaded returning to those who had sent him.

Something like this would explain not only Paul's threefold reference to the extremity of his illness (noted above) but also the fulsome way he introduces his remarks about the man. He is a "brother" (a fellow Christian), a "fellow-worker" (deeply committed to Paul's mission), and a "fellow-soldier." Paul only uses the latter word on one other occasion.[55] Because Philippi was famous for a great battle (in 42 BC) and a base for retired military men, it may be Paul's way of saying that Epaphroditus was a brave soldier of Christ.

As well, Paul notes that Epaphroditus is their *messenger* (literally, "apostle") whom they had sent to Paul as their *minister* to his *needs*.[56] Epaphroditus brought the Philippians' gift of money to Rome, and probably planned to attend to Paul's day-to-day needs in prison, for example, the provision of clean clothes and food, but above all spiritual support.

---

55. Phlm 2.
56. Phil 2:25.

Paul begins this passage by asserting it was *his* decision to send Epaphroditus home. This desperately sick man was keen to stay, but it was Paul's insistence that he return to Philippi. For his part Epaphroditus was deeply concerned that news of his illness had reached Philippi (we do not know how).

Accordingly, Paul was keen to send Epaphroditus back to Philippi so that the people will "rejoice at seeing him again." Therefore, he requests, "receive him in the Lord with all joy and honor such a man who nearly died for the work of Christ." He risked his life "to complete what was lacking in your service to me," that is, he was the Philippians' proxy, doing for them on their behalf what they could not directly do for Paul.

Beyond saving Epaphroditus from shame at his failed mission, there was another reason for Paul's strong encouragement to "receive him in the Lord with all joy." Epaphroditus was most probably also the source of information about local problems that Paul now addresses in the letter.

It is obvious that Paul was a deep thinker, a rigorous polemicist, and a stalwart for high moral standards in the churches. His words about Epaphroditus tell us that he was aware of the real life situation in Philippi and that acted out of pastoral diplomacy to shield the man who had come to help him.

Paul's Mission and Christian Origins

Our survey of Paul's coworkers opens a window that reveals the extent of Paul's mission from ca. AD 34–65. Throughout those three decades Paul established churches in five Roman provinces, recruited mission associates, and wrote numerous letters.

In other words, the former Pharisee and persecutor began his vigorous missions within just a few years of Jesus' ministry lifespan (ca. AD 29–33). As noted, his letters indicate that the intellectual foundation of these churches was the traditions (theological, liturgical, and ethical) that he delivered to them. Paul received many of these key traditions, which were already preformulated and preformatted, most probably in Jerusalem in the brief period between the end of Jesus in AD 33 and Paul's return to the holy city in ca. AD 37.

This observation has profound implications for the question of Christian origins. Paul's missions began almost back-to-back with the historical Jesus. Only about four years marked the end of Jesus' lifespan and the beginning of Paul's missions in Syria-Cilicia. The only satisfactory explanation for Paul's missions is the impact of the historical Jesus on the formation of traditions in Jerusalem that Paul used as the doctrinal and liturgical bedrock for his churches.

Conclusion

Paul's immense missionary achievement occurred over a relatively short period of time. This would not have been possible without the loyal help of a significant group of coworkers.

We have focused our attention on Silvanus, a skillful translator; Timothy, a loyal surrogate son; Luke, a meticulous historian; Priscilla and Aquila, initiative-taking leaders; Philemon, a gifted evangelist; Titus, a loyal ambassador; Phoebe a generous hostess; and Epaphroditus, a brave carer.

With the help of these and other loyal and able coworkers Paul established a network of churches in the provinces that ringed the Aegean Sea and thereby laid the foundation of the Christian Empire in the east, centered on Constantinople. Each of these was loyal to Paul while also being gifted leaders in their own right.

Eleven

The Importance of Membership

PAUL GATHERED THOSE WHO responded to his message about the Son of God into congregations. We ask, why? Why didn't he call on hearers to acknowledge Jesus privately, as it were, and leave them to get on with their lives? But he does not. Paul's letters assume that believers would attend church meetings.

Let me suggest five reasons.

First, church membership provided for the "up-building" of the individual member, but also of the church itself. Paul frequently uses the noun *oikodomē* and its verb to urge the "construction" of Christian belief and ethics within the church. Paul's was an architectural metaphor for the rising maturity of individuals and the faith community. It was an apt metaphor on account of the large amount of contemporary construction—temples, aqueducts, arenas, stately mansions—under construction in the *Pax Romana*.

The repetition of gospel teaching was directed to the up-building of the individual and of the congregation. The critical test for all activities in church meetings was this up-building in Christian spiritual and ethical maturity. If an activity did not "build up" the church in mature Christianity it had no place at the meeting.[1]

The pervasive Greco-Roman culture powerfully confirmed its people in ungodly behavior. The church meeting was critically important to secure the alternative spiritual and ethical worldview that Paul had introduced.

---

1. 1 Cor 14:12.

The Importance of Membership

Second, church membership provided the opportunity to exercise and receive love-inspired ministry. This is especially clear from 1 Corinthians.

Roman colonies like Corinth were deeply stratified along the lines of rank and wealth. In the church, however, there was—according to Paul—a distribution of ministry gifts unrelated to one's social place within the city. According to Paul, "to *each* is given the manifestation of the Spirit for the *common* good."[2] While Paul teaches a descending hierarchy of the usefulness of the gifts, these were quite independent of the rank, or lack of rank, among the members.[3] In fact, Paul observes, there were few notable people within the church.[4]

The truly important thing was that the use of the gifts was to be motivated by love (*agapē*) for the other members. This prompts Paul to write his famous chapter on love in 1 Cor 13. In that chapter we hear the words of Paul the diplomatic pastor. To this point the letter has been a succession of examples of the *failure* of love within the congregation, as for example, in the members' factiousness, litigiousness, the selfishness of the rich toward the poor at the Remembrance Meal, and the self-seeking display of gifts during the church meeting.

For Paul, then, the church was the place to act lovingly for the welfare of others and, not least, to receive that love. "Bear one another's burdens," he wrote elsewhere, "and so fulfill the law of Christ."[5]

He referred to a church as a spiritual family composed of "brothers and sisters." These sibling-relationships cut across and were independent of family relationships within the city. The Greeks had an ideal of "brotherly love" as reflected in a number of cities named in honor of that love, Philadelphia. Paul's vision for the church, whose members had been blessed with the Holy Spirit, was to be a true "Philadelphia."

Third, church membership provided a glimpse of the glorious future. Paul saw a congregation as a new society, as for example, in words like "body" and "commonwealth" we find in his letters that also appeared in the writings of the political theorists.

For centuries in the Greco-Roman world philosophers and statesmen had struggled to define the ideal society. Socrates's dialogues as recorded in Plato's *Republic*, for example, looked for the just state ruled by a

---

2. 1 Cor 12:7.
3. 1 Cor 12:27–30.
4. 1 Cor 1:26.
5. Gal 6:2.

philosopher-king. Alexander the Great sought to implement *homonoia*—harmony—between disparate peoples like the Macedonians, other Greeks, and the Persians. Cicero saw "concordia" (Latin version of *homonoia*) realized in an informed citizenship ruled by a wise senate, but threatened by ruthless warlords like Pompey and Julius Caesar. In fact, Cicero's dream was shattered by decades of civil war until Augustus emerged victorious as the sole leader at the Battle of Actium in 31 BC.

Paul would not have been unaware of theories for the conduct of society. His visit to Antioch in Pisidia in ca. AD 48 confronted him with a copy of Augustus's famous *Res Gestae* ("Things done") and his claims to have made Rome great. Paul would also have known of the visit to Tarsus in 41 BC of civil war protagonists, Antony and Cleopatra.

Paul inculcated another vision in his congregations.

> There is neither Jew nor Greek, there is neither slave nor free, there is no male and female, for you are all one in Christ Jesus. And if you are Christ's, then you are Abraham's offspring, heirs according to promise.[6]

> So then you are no longer strangers and aliens, but you are fellow citizens with the saints and members of the household of God.[7]

> Here there is not Greek and Jew, circumcised and uncircumcised, barbarian, Scythian, slave, free; but Christ is all, and in all.[8]

Paul refers to significant divisions in the Greco-Roman world:

Between Jews and Greeks (i.e., gentiles)	Gal 3:28
Between free people and slaves	Gal 3:28
Between males and females	Gal 3:28
Between Greeks and Barbarians	Rom 1:14

There were other divisions:

Between Roman citizens and non-citizens

Between the wealthy and powerful and the poor and weak

Between "patrons" and "clients"

---

6. Gal 3:28–29.
7. Eph 2:19.
8. Col 3:11.

The Importance of Membership

This body of people "in Christ" was not merely a here-and-now social construct. A church was to anticipate God's *end-time* "commonwealth." This is one reason Paul was so bitterly critical of current ego-inspired divisions within his congregations. For such divisions made the churches no better than the countries divided by ego-driven politicians and warlords who for years had wrought havoc in the Roman world.

Paul often spoke of the hope to be held and enjoyed by individual believers. But he was equally concerned for their *corporate* hope, the heavenly communion of the end-time.

> Having the eyes of your hearts enlightened, that you may know what is the hope to which he has called you, what are the riches of his glorious inheritance in the saints.[9]

Fourth, church membership was a "nursery" for growth in the likeness of Christ. Paul was the spiritual father of the members of the churches he had founded. Many times he calls on his children to imitate him.

> I became your father in Christ through the gospel. I urge you, then, be imitators of me.[10]

The ultimate pattern or template for congregants, however, was not Paul, but Christ.

> Be imitators of me, as I am of Christ.[11]

Paul's vision was that the members would imitate Christ in their dealings with one another. He repeatedly points to the example of Christ.

- To encourage sacrificial generosity:

> For you know the grace of our Lord Jesus Christ, that though he was rich, yet for your sake he became poor, so that you by his poverty might become rich.[12]

- To encourage respectful humility:

> Let each of you look not only to his own interests, but also to the interests of others. Have this mind among yourselves, which is yours in Christ Jesus, who, though he was in the form of God, did

---

9. Eph 1:18.
10. 1 Cor 4:15–16 (also 2 Cor 6:13; Phil 3:17).
11. 1 Cor 11:1.
12. 2 Cor 8:9.

not count equality with God a thing to be grasped, but emptied himself, by taking the form of a servant.[13]

- To encourage the reciprocal welcome of one another:

  May the God of endurance and encouragement grant you to live in . . . harmony with one another, in accord with Christ Jesus. . . . Therefore welcome one another as Christ has welcomed you, for the glory of God.[14]

- To seek the salvation of others:

  I try to please everyone in everything I do, not seeking my own advantage, but that of many, that they may be saved. Be imitators of me, as I am of Christ.[15]

Paul taught extensively about the life, values, and behavior of Jesus. He sought the practical imitation of his Lord in the many and varied aspects of life.

Fifth, church was a place where the outsider was welcome. Although the churches typically met in private homes, non-members (Greek, *idiōtai*) were welcome to attend. We do not know whether their attendance was by invitation or by an open door to the home of the host. What is clear from 1 Corinthians was the concern not to give the visitor a false impression of Christian values. If the members spoke in "tongues" that were not explained, the outsider would conclude that the church meeting was a madhouse, and be deflected from further interest in the message about Christ.[16]

For these and related reasons Paul expected those who were baptized in the name of Christ to belong to a gathering of people he called "the body of Christ." The church was a society of spiritual equals where they could offer and receive love, and to make progress in doctrinal and ethical understanding.

---

13. Phil 2:4–7.
14. Rom 15:5–7.
15. 1 Cor 10:33—11:1.
16. 1 Cor 14:23.

Perception of Churches

How would people have classified the churches? We are curious to know what the people in the Greco-Roman cities thought of these gatherings. They would have been struck by how different they were from other meetings of people. They were not like temples to the gods, with priests offering sacrifices. Indeed, they were called "atheists" because they did not believe in the gods.

They were not secret groups like the various mystery cults—of Cybele, Orpheus, Dionysius, or Isis; noninitiated *outsiders* attended. Both Tacitus and Pliny refer to the Christians as a *superstitio*, a sect that stood aloof from Caesar worship.

Sources external to and hostile to the Christians (Josephus and Tacitus) don't cast much light on their actual activities. Pliny informed Trajan that the Christians sang a hymn to Christ as if a god, and bound one another to observe certain ethical standards.

Outsiders would probably have seen the church meeting as a kind of synagogue. Like synagogues the churches read, listened to, and received homilies on *written* texts. Unlike the synagogues, however, the church liturgy was less rigid and there was considerable verbal activity by ordinary members.

Twelve

Paul's Spiritual World

PAUL WAS NOT A modern man. His view of the world was very different from our modern, secular view. In this chapter, we attempt to understand how Paul saw the cosmos around him.

Paul's Worldview

Paul often uses the word "world," for example, "Do not be conformed to this world."[1] Here, though, Paul's actual word is *aeon* or "age." It is an extended period of *time*, not a geographical reference. If we think of the world as the creation it is "good . . . very good" according to Gen 1, but the *aeon* is not good. Paul refers to it as "this present *evil aeon*."[2]

"This *aeon*" began with our first parents' rebellion against their loving Creator and their exclusion from the Garden of Eden. From that time the human race has suffered three problems: first, its continued rebellion against God; second, its blind worship of the creation instead of the Creator; and third, the universal reality of death.

Regarding the first, Paul writes that in this present *aeon* all humanity is "under sin," as if "sin" was an evil giant standing over us with his heel on our throats.[3] This is as true for Jews who have the law of God (but do not keep it) as it is for non-Jews who have the law of conscience (but act against

1. Rom 12:2.
2. Gal 1:4.
3. Rom 3:9.

it). Paul concluded that "all (Jews and gentiles) have sinned and continue to fall short of the glory of God."[4]

Our second problem, according to Paul, is that humanity is blind to the Creator and focuses its mind instead on the creation. This is because "the god of this *aeon* has blinded the minds of the unbelievers to keep them from seeing the light of the gospel of the glory of Christ."[5] The people of this *aeon* are deceived and misled by its god, who is God's enemy, the devil.

Because of this spiritual "blindness" the peoples of the world illogically worship what is created rather than the one, true, living God who created all things. Idolatry is illogical because men and women, who are intellectually superior to mindless objects, fall down and worship mindless, lifeless pieces of wood or stone.[6] For this false worship humanity is culpable, without excuse, and subject to the just judgment of God.[7]

Death, which Paul calls "the last enemy," is humanity's third problem.[8] Death is the direct consequence of its rebellion. "Just as sin came into the world through one man, and death through sin, and so death spread to all men because all sinned."[9] God will destroy "the last enemy" but until he does it rules like a tyrant over everybody within this *aeon*.

Paul lived at the height of the classical age, the climax of a thousand years of Greek philosophy, science, history, and drama writing. It was also the acme of Roman military might and of Rome's architectural and engineering achievements. The Greeks and the Romans had displayed remarkable cleverness in their mundane achievements but were foolish in matters of ultimate importance. They venerated the gods, an act of folly, but refused to turn to the Creator.

Greek and Roman culture was steeped in immorality, as their own thinkers recognized, but were helpless to correct. Part of the problem was that the gods they worshipped were immoral, which in turn sanctioned the immorality of their worshippers.

Paul often refers to human immorality and gives lists of vices. But these were a symptom of a deeper problem, their refusal to worship and

---

4. Rom 3:23.
5. 2 Cor 4:4.
6. Rom 1:18–23.
7. Rom 1:20.
8. 1 Cor 15:26.
9. Rom 5:12.

thank the Creator and their determination to worship the gods. Paul, however, was not a moralist whose mission was to curb immorality.

Not surprisingly, Paul refers to "the wisdom of this age"—that approves of idolatry—as folly (literally "moronic").[10] The worship of created *things* is plainly foolish.

Rather, Paul proclaimed the true "wisdom of God" in the message of the crucified Son of God.[11] That message did two things. It exposed the folly of the "wisdom of this age" and it revealed God's true "wisdom," which is Christ crucified, through whom God forgives sins. The true "wisdom of God" is the message of his crucified Son that destroys any notion of human reason as a way to find God or give access to the *aeon* of *aeons*.

The *aeon* will conclude at the end of history, as ordained by God. When this *aeon* ends it will inaugurate the *aeon* of *aeons*, often referred to as "forever" and sometimes thought of as "eternity." It is not timeless, however, but a new kind of time when God's blessings will never end.

This was Paul's worldview.

Modern Worldview

Modern wisdom is entirely secular and God-less and leaves the Almighty out of any discussion about the world, science, or morality. The passing of the years from antiquity to modernity has not fundamentally changed human attitudes to the Creator. People are as uninterested in the almighty Creator today as they were in Paul's day.

Like the Greeks and Romans, the achievements of modern people are stunning, especially in science and technology. But these are morally neutral and can be instruments of good or evil. Photography can help recall special family moments or transmit pornography.

Morality takes a step forward and then a step back. We install ramps for wheelchair use, and we take elaborate precautions to prevent identity theft. Progress is balanced by regress.

---

10. 1 Cor 2:6.
11. 1 Cor 1:21.

Paul's World and Ours

Modern language about our world is different from Paul's but the reality is not dissimilar. Blindness to God the Creator is as real now as it was back then. Television personalities produce visually brilliant programs about wildlife and nature but attribute their beauty and intricacy to a mindless, impersonal force, evolution or "mother nature." In effect, they attribute our complex, beautiful world to "blind chance," which is a form of idolatry. To utter the name of God or attribute the glory of nature to an intelligent, transcendent being is secular blasphemy, the ultimate in political incorrectness.

We tend not to attribute wrongdoing to the devil, but—for example—to individuals with disadvantaged childhoods. Somehow, *they* are the victims of the crimes they commit against truly innocent victims.

Occasionally, however, acts of such gratuitous cruelty and chilling malice confront us that we are driven to describe them as "pure evil," so unimaginably wicked are they. These are not uncommon but appear almost nightly on our TV screens. They lead us to attribute them to supra human evil, even to the devil. Consider the evils of Auschwitz, perpetrated by educated, Mozart-loving men who played with their children at night.

In fact, the daily news—whether in print media or electronic media—is mostly bad news. The "news" is a continual reminder of ineradicable evil among us.

Historically, informed political leaders understand that evil is a reality, a given, one that will not diminish, for example, with greater education. They know that evil is to be *restrained* and that a society needs an alert police force, judicial process for adjudicating criminal acts, and prisons for the guilty. Equally they are aware of the need for a defense force as a deterrent against foreign incursion.

In other words, our political systems and investment of large budgetary items indirectly confirm the ongoing presence of evil in our world.

Thirteen

Paul and the Christian Mind

Paul's Church Meetings

PAUL'S CHURCH MEETINGS WERE not recognizably "religious" or "cultic." That may have been true of the mystery religions of that era, but it was not true of the gathering of believers in Paul's mission. True, there was strong emphasis on prayer—whether thanksgiving or intercession—but also as ascription to God for his inestimable moral qualities.

These meetings were precisely that, "meetings," for that is what the word "church" (*ekklēsia*) meant. It was a secular word not a religious one, as Acts 19 demonstrates. In verses 32 and 41 this word was used for the people *assembled* in the theater and in verse 39 for a *meeting* of the city parliament. The Christians did not gather in temples or other designated religious places but in ordinary homes.

The primary function of the church meeting was not religious but educational, the imparting and receiving of morally and theologically tinged knowledge for the purpose of edification, that is, the moral and spiritual up-building of those who gathered.

This understanding emerges from Paul's directions to the Corinthian Christians who had become unhelpfully preoccupied by a religious and mystical activity, *glossolalia*, "speaking in tongues." In Paul's mind the Corinthians had become too "religious," although Paul doesn't use that term. Paul emphatically downplayed the Corinthians' fascination with this novelty.

In church I would rather speak five words with my *mind* in order to *instruct* others, than ten thousand words in a tongue.[1]

Paul explains what he means by "words."

When you come together, each one has a hymn, a lesson (a teaching), a revelation, a tongue, or an interpretation. Let all things be done for building up.[2]

These various words must fulfill the edification test, including "a tongue," which must be interpreted (i.e., explained). In the same chapter he wrote, "strive to excel in *building up* the church,"[3] that is, by the application of words that are understood.

True, the practice of the sacraments of baptism and the Lord's Supper were *symbolic,* word-free acts that could be regarded as religious. But their setting was mundane and their message self-evident. Baptisms occurred in ordinary waterways and the Lord's Supper was embedded in an evening meal in a home. The former spelled the end of the old way of life and the beginning of the new, and the latter was a corporate remembering of the Lord's death.

Since church life, therefore, was directed to the "building up" of the mind, we are not surprised that Paul should place so much emphasis on "thinking."

Encouragement to the Philippian Christians

Toward the end of his letter to the Philippians Paul reveals the things he "thinks" about. He does so in the manner of a rabbi who encourages his disciples to imitate his way of life.

Philippians 4

8 Finally, brothers,
whatever is true,
whatever is honorable,
whatever is just,
whatever is pure,

---

1. 1 Cor 14:19.
2. 1 Cor 14:26.
3. 1 Cor 14:12.

> whatever is lovely,
> whatever is commendable,
> if there is any excellence,
> if there is anything worthy of praise,
> *think* about these things.
> 9 What you have learned and received and heard and seen in me
> —practise these things—
> and the God of peace will be with you.

This is one of Paul's most rhetorically balanced texts. Perhaps he crafted it in keeping with the sophisticated culture of Philippi, "the leading city of the district of Macedonia and a Roman colony" (Acts 16:12). Paul achieved the rhetorical impact by a fivefold repetition of "whatever is," followed by his twofold "if there is any . . ." and concluded by a twofold direction to "think" and "practise." It is an elegant and powerful text.

At that time there was an interest in the use of single words to convey moral virtues. Inscribed on the plinth of the Library of Celsus in Ephesus are the words "wisdom," "virtue," and "intellect." People of that era were drawn to the three graces ("charm," "beauty," and "creativity") that were portrayed as three beautiful young women. Caesar Augustus' shield bore the words "virtue," "mercy," "justice," and "duty."

It is striking that articulation of these virtues belonged to the upper echelons of Greco-Roman society, which was sharply stratified. The wealthy and powerful were a minority and these words applied to them, and not to the strata below them, including to the slaves at the bottom of the social pyramid. These words are elitist in application.

Paul, too, used single words but they were not the words of his contemporaries in that culture. Rather, they were words that echoed the Bible and the developing gospel-tradition, and they applied to all church members, rich and poor, male and female, slave and free.

The first four words relate to *inner* qualities, that is to say, attitudes. "Whatever is *true*" echoes Paul's reference to the gospel as the "open statement of the *truth*;"[4] "whatever is *honorable*" is similar to Paul's concern for an elder's "serious behavior";[5] "whatever is *just*" captures the vision of God

---

4. 2 Cor 4:2; 6:7.
5. Titus 2:2.

who is "just" and the source of "justice";[6] and "whatever is pure" is an ideal for a virgin.[7]

The remaining two things to "think about" are external in character: "whatever is *lovely*"; "whatever—that is, *whoever*—is *commendable*" ("of good reputation").[8] "Whatever is lovely" refers to *things* (music, art, architecture) whereas "whatever is commendable" refers to *people*, who are decent and good. Perhaps Paul is echoing the Creator's verdict of his creation that it was "good . . . very good."[9]

When Paul writes "if there is any excellence, if there is anything worthy of praise, *think* about these things," he is calling for discernment, for an active moral discrimination.

Discernment was important in the world of Paul. At a superficial level the great cities like Philippi were culturally advanced, with well-designed and carefully constructed public buildings. At the same time the wealthy and powerful kept the lower orders and slaves in their vice-like grip. Slaves who stepped out of line were crucified. People and animals were killed as public entertainment. Superstition was rife. Many people worshipped rocks, believed plants could be deities, owned sacred animals, accepted ritual castration and prostitution. Excessive drinking was common and it was believed that the gods (*daemons*) spoke through the slurred speech of the inebriated. Pedophilia was common involving adult males and boys at symposia (drinking parties).

Paul, however, does not write to condemn the moral failures of society but rather calls on Christians to adopt a morally discriminating attitude toward it as a basis for maintaining a safe distance from it.

Upon reflection, each positive attitude that the Christian reader is to think about implies a negative attitude that is to be avoided. To think about what is *true, honorable, just, pure* implies the rejection of what is *untrue, dishonorable, unjust,* and *impure*. In other words, the list of things to think about has a deeply moral tone.

---

6. Rom 3:26.
7. 2 Cor 11:2.
8. 2 Cor 6:8.
9. Gen 1:31.

The Thinking Person

Paul is holding before the Philippians the ideal of a thinking person whose attitudes are shaped by gospel values that in turn approve "*whatever* is lovely" and "*whoever* is commendable." This is liberating, for it means that the discriminating Christian can appreciate music, literature, and art so long as it is measured by God's standards of excellence. Likewise it means the Christian can value worthy and decent people whether or not they are fellow believers.

These verses smash the stereotype of Paul as a grim Philistine who was opposed to every aspect of human culture.

Paul sums up his list of six good attitudes by "if there is any excellence . . . anything worthy of praise, think about *these things*." If these were fulfilled, the person would be morally motivated but also engaged with the world and society in which they lived.

Remarkably, Paul saw these things as aspirations of his own life. These six attitudes (four internal and moral; two external and aesthetic) reveal *his* mind to his readers, regarding the things *he* "thinks about." Not only does Paul reveal his inner self to his readers, he goes so far as to position himself as the template to things for them to think about and put into practice—"what you have *learned* and *received* and *heard* and *seen* in me—practise *these* things."

This is the vocabulary of a rabbi who invites his disciples to learn from the master, but also to emulate his total life. Let them recall not only his words but also what manner of man Paul was when present with them. Paul's self-portrait is of a man whose mind was steeped in biblical values, but who could admire beautiful things and commend praiseworthy people.

Paul's Benediction

Paul concludes this passage with an implied benediction: "the God of peace will be with you." God, whose character is "peace," imparts his peace ("the God of peace will be with you") as you think about and put into practice the six items in this list.

The mind that is filled with the antitheses of these six good things will not be a mind at peace, but in turmoil, fear, and rage. The God of peace imparts the peace of God to those who "make their requests known" to God and who think about and do those things that are morally and aesthetically good.

The words of Phil 4:8–9 appears as the motto on the coat of arms of the BBC, which in turn inspired these words on the entrance of Broadcasting House.

> This Temple of the Arts and Muses is dedicated to Almighty God by the first Governors of Broadcasting House in the year 1931, Sir John Reith being Director-General. It is their prayer that good seed sown may bring forth a good harvest, that all things hostile to peace or purity may be banished from this house, and that the people, inclining their ear to whatsoever things are beautiful and honest and of good report, may tread the path of wisdom and uprightness.

Those lofty words are testimony to the wisdom and goodness of the apostle Paul.

Fourteen

Paul's Concerns

ANYONE READING PAUL'S LETTERS knows that he was very concerned that his churches believed the right things and behaved in the right ways. In this chapter we will think about four evils that Paul addressed: legalism, libertinism, elitism, and triumphalism.

Legalism

For his first thirty years Paul the Jew had attempted to "live to God" by keeping the tenets of the law of Moses. Paul, however, knew in the depths of his being that he did not fulfill that law, and that as a consequence he did not really know God in a personal way. Outside Damascus Paul came to understand that faith in Jesus crucified and not works of the law was the way to "live to God," in fact the only way.

God directed Paul to preach this message "among the gentiles" and this he proceeded to do, first in Arabia and then in the province of Syria-Cilicia. In AD 48 he brought this message to the high plateau country of southern Galatia and established a network of churches there. This came to the attention of conservative Jewish Christians in Jerusalem who launched a counter-mission among the Galatian churches. Their aim was to require the gentile members to fulfill the works of the law, including male circumcision and the observation of the Jewish religious calendar.

Back in Antioch Paul wrote his letter to the Galatians urging them to cherish their freedom in Christ and not submit to the yoke of slavery. Soon afterward the counter-mission also came to the churches in Syria-Cilicia,

Paul's Concerns

including to the church in Antioch, where they attempted to impose Jewish food laws and male circumcision on gentile Christians.[1] To attempt to resolve this crisis a conference was held in AD 49 in Jerusalem that decided in favor of Paul's teaching on freedom for non-Jewish Christians.

The depth of Jewish conservatism in Jerusalem was such, however, that counter-missions continued to go forth seeking to impose the works of the law on the gentile members of Paul's churches.

It wasn't that the anti-Paul movement was always coordinated. Their attempts to "correct" Paul's theology in Galatia, Syria-Cilicia, and Corinth were the result of intentionally planned missions from Jerusalem. The attempts to impose circumcision on gentiles in Rome and Philippi, however, seem to have arisen locally rather than from Jerusalem. Nevertheless, the international Jewish network was extensive and Jewish Christians often continued as part of that network. Paul suffered from hostile and negative opinion from Jews everywhere, including from Jews who were Christians.

The result was that Paul was often forced to defend the principle and practice of spiritual freedom against the demands of Jewish Christian legalism. This certainly was the dominant message of Galatians, 2 Corinthians, Romans, and Philippians.

These words capture Paul's passion for "freedom" that was so precious to him and which he vigorously defended for his churches:

> For freedom Christ has set us free; stand firm therefore and do not submit again to a *yoke* of slavery.[2]

These words echo Jesus's words to his original disciples whom the Pharisees were seeking to coerce as strict observers of the law:

> Come to me, all who labor and are heavy laden, and I will give you rest. Take my *yoke* upon you, and learn from me, for I am gentle and lowly in heart, and you will find rest to your souls.[3]

It is probably not a coincidence that Paul used the word "yoke," as Jesus also had.

Grace, not legalism opens the door to a personal relationship with God. This was deeply part of the message of Paul, the servant of Jesus.

---

1. Acts 15:1; Gal 2:11–14.
2. Gal 5:1.
3. Matt 11:28–29.

Libertinism

In Corinth some of the Christians were demanding the opposite of legalism, total freedom. Their catch cry was: "All things are lawful to me."[4]

Some of the Corinthian Christians believed they were free to visit the local temple prostitutes and to eat food that had previously been sacrificed to the gods. (All food was offered to the gods in the temple. Part was then eaten by the priests and the remainder sold in the shops. For Jews this food was "unclean.")

How did the Corinthians arrive at the libertarian understanding that "all things are lawful"? In part, this extreme version of personal freedom was part of Greek culture. However, it probably arose more directly from a misunderstanding of Christian freedom that said, "I am free to do anything I like."

Note Paul's pointed words, "All things are lawful to me," which matches "*Each* one of you says, '*I* follow x, y, or z'" (1 Cor 1:12). The words "I" and "me" reflect extreme, self-centered individualism.

This blinded them from recognizing obvious wrongdoing like visiting a prostitute in pagan temples (which doubled as brothels). Also, it hindered them from responding in a sensitive way to the delicate issue of eating idol-sacrificed food in the home of an unbeliever.[5]

Theoretically a Christian is free in conscience to eat any food—idol-sacrificed or not—but that situation changes when the believer is in the home of an unbeliever.

If the issue is raised in the course of the meal then the Christian will decline to eat lest his host is confirmed in the rightness of idol-worship. What these Corinthian libertines did not understand was that Christian freedom is not a permission to engage *in* wrongdoing but the power from God to be free *from* wrongdoing, and to be free to be a loving, others-centered person.

While Paul resisted the imposition of "works of the law" on gentile believers (like male circumcision) he insisted that the Ten Commandments were the ongoing basis for Christian morality.

> For neither circumcision counts for anything, nor uncircumcision, but keeping the commandments of God.[6]

---

4. 1 Cor 6:12; 10:23.
5. 1 Cor 10:23.
6. 1 Cor 7:19.

Paul retained those commandments as the revelation of God's will. Rather than restate them in negative terms ("Thou shalt not"), however, he expressed them as positive examples of one's love of neighbor. He wrote that each commandment is summed up in this word: "You shall love your neighbor as yourself."[7]

Of special interest is his approach to the commandment against stealing:

> Let the thief no longer steal, but rather let him labor, doing honest work with his own hands, so that he may have something to share with anyone in need.[8]

Paul restates the negative commandment as a positive encouragement, one that has a loving outcome, working to care for those in need.

Elitism

Roman colonies like Corinth and Philippi were miniature versions of the mother city, Rome. In that city, and in her colonies, wealth was sought after because it provided the resources to buy influence. For example, the capacity to secure the loyalty of the legions was connected with the capacity of politicians to pay them handsomely. Money plus military success vaulted them to become *Imperators*.

Wealthy men, urged on by their ambitious wives, engaged in fierce competition for political honors, for example to be elected to the senate, including to the highest office as a consul. This was as true in the colonies as it was in Rome. Competitive politics for honored recognition in elections was a core activity in Corinth and Philippi.

Those at the pinnacle of wealth employed their money to bestow favors on those who belonged to the next levels down, who in turn patronized those below them. Those who gave favors expected loyalty in return to advance the patron's political aspirations. This was a ritualized form of friendship called *amicitia*, but it was a ruthless, demanding "friendship" not an unconditional friendship as taught by Paul. Failure to observe the conventions of *amicitia* inspired enmity, relentless hatred.

---

7. Rom 13:9.
8. Eph 4:28.

Inevitably the culture of elitism and competition as expressed in patronage resulted in division and conflict between ambitious individuals and families. Political strife was commonplace in Rome and her colonies.

The faith communities in Corinth and Philippi were not unaffected by the secular values of these cities and their quarrelsome culture.

A spirit of competition between leading church members is evident in Paul's letters to these churches. In Corinth this was manifested in the proponents of the various missionaries who had visited Corinth, Paul, Apollos, and Cephas. In Philippi socially prominent women, Euodia and Syntyche, appear to have been vying with one another for the loyalty of the members. In Corinth the spirit of competition even extended to the quest for the recognition of one's superior gifts.[9]

The competitive attitudes of members issued in two unhelpful consequences.

One was that their rivalry resulted in a loss of unity within the wider church community. Paul refers to social quarrelling among the Corinthians, but also to spiritual division during the church meeting.[10] Paul chides the Philippians for their "rivalry and conceit."[11]

The other was the marginalizing of lesser members. The highmindedness of socially elite members in Corinth provoked Paul to remind them that they were "not many."[12] He sharply rebuked the "haves" for their shameful failure to share with the "have nots" at the thanksgiving meal.[13] His words, "The eye cannot say to the hand 'I have no need of you,'" and his assurance "If one member suffers, all suffer" were directed to those who felt their gifts made them so spiritually superior that it was as if there were no other gifts except theirs.

In other words, both 1 Corinthians and Philippians imply that the competitiveness and elitism in Roman cities had been replicated within the churches in Corinth and Philippi. Paul, the servant of Christ, who was a humble tent maker, took the part of those socially and spiritually lesser members of the churches.

It is highly significant that the arrogance of the elites in both churches inspired two of Paul's most famous pieces of writing, the chapter on love in

---

9. 1 Cor 12:7.
10. 1 Cor 1:11; 12:25.
11. Phil 1:27; 2:3, 14.
12. 1 Cor 2:26.
13. 1 Cor 11:21–22.

1 Corinthians and the passage on Christ's humility as a crucified slave in Philippians. Both of these wonderfully lyrical passages are directed to loveless, arrogant elitism. Elitism—socioeconomic or spiritual—has no place in the body of Christ and we have Paul to thank for his powerful teaching to dispel it.

Triumphalism

Paul would have confronted triumphalism as a Pharisee and as a Roman citizen.

Paul the Pharisee

In Jesus' parable of the Pharisee and tax collector he exposed the religious triumphalism and sense of superiority of the Pharisees. The Pharisee, standing by himself, prayed thus:

> God, I thank you that I am not like other men, extortioners, unjust, adulterers, or even like this tax collector.[14]

We hear the Pharisee Paul's own sense of high achievement in his *Curriculum Vitae*:

> If anyone else thinks he has reason for confidence in the flesh, I have *more*: circumcised on the eighth day, of the people of Israel, of the tribe of Benjamin, a Hebrew of Hebrews; as to the law a Pharisee; as to zeal, a persecutor of the church; as to righteousness under the law, blameless.[15]

When he became a man "in Christ," however, he saw himself differently:

> But whatever gain I had, I counted as loss for the sake of Christ. Indeed, I count everything as loss because of the surpassing worth of knowing Christ Jesus my Lord.[16]

What changed Paul's heart from his sense of superiority to realistic humility? It was because at and since Damascus he had been spiritually

14. Luke 18:11.
15. Phil 3:5–7.
16. Phil 3:7–8.

united with the crucified but resurrected Christ. Paul uses the language of "boasting," not on account of his achievements, but only in the kindness and strength of God. Echoing Jer 9:24 Paul writes, "Let the one who boasts, boast in the Lord."[17]

Paul the Roman Citizen

Paul was by birth (in ca. AD 5) a Roman citizen, which meant that even as a boy he was conscious of social superiority over others in Syria-Cilicia, his home province. His years in Jerusalem (ca. AD 17–34) were dominated by Jewish scholarship and temple worship, and would have meant minimal contact with Roman culture and practice. Once he returned to the province of Syria-Cilicia (ca. AD 37–47), however, he was once more located in a Roman environment. This was especially true of his time in Antioch, capital of Syria-Cilicia, a Roman garrison city.

Exposure to Roman culture was to intensify once his westward mission journeys began. In ca. AD 47 he had a close engagement with the Sergius Paulus, proconsul of Cyprus. Luke states that from that time Saul was known as "Paul," a Roman name, probably adopted in honor of Sergius Paulus.

Paul travelled from Cyprus up through the mountains to Antioch in Pisidia, an important Roman colony located at the major Roman military crossroads from west to east and from north to south.

Here, most probably for the first time, Paul encountered pronounced Roman triumphalism. In 25 BC, a mere six years after Augustus won the battle of Actium that gave him sole control of the Roman Empire, the city became a Roman colony. Its name, *Colonia Caesarea*, honored Caesar Augustus. The city was divided into five "vici," districts, as in Rome. By coincidence the city had seven high points, corresponding with seven hills of the Eternal City. Most surviving inscriptions are in Latin, although the spoken language was Greek.

Clearly Antioch was a major city, having between 100,000 and 150,000 inhabitants, among them many retired legionaires.

Memory of Caesar Augustus dominated the city. The temple to Augustus, built shortly after his death in AD 14, was the city's most imposing building located at its pinnacle. One of the two city squares was dedicated to Augustus. The triple vaulted *Propylon* (monumental outer gate to the

---

17. 1 Cor 1:31.

temple) was inscribed with the name AUGUSTUS. It was dedicated to him and decorated with statues and symbols of his sea victory at Actium, celebrating his victory and triumph.

Equally significantly, inscribed on the Propylon at eye level was Augustus's self-written funeral eulogy, *Res Gestae Divi Augusti* ("Things done by the deified Augustus"). Augustus began, "Below is a copy of the acts of the deified Augustus by which he placed the whole world under the sovereignty of the Roman people, and the amounts he expended upon the state and the Roman people."

What follows, written in the first person, is Augustus's list of political and military achievements, including the creation of numerous colonies. At no point does Augustus admit to any failure or concede any defeat.

On the reasonable assumption that Paul the Roman citizen could read Latin we conclude that Paul could have read the *Res Gestae* during his three known visits to *Colonia Caesarea*.

We can imagine that the impact on Paul in his visits to Pisidian Antioch was overwhelming. It spoke to him of proud achievement and the exalted place accorded to Caesar Augustus. By contrast, the king whom Paul served was the humble servant of God, whom the Romans crucified. If the Caesar was the embodiment of raw power, the Christ of the gospel was the incarnation of humility and self-sacrificing service.

It is almost certain that Paul reacted against Roman triumphalism with Christian anti-triumphalism.

Some years later when he was confronting elitism in Roman Corinth, he portrayed himself as a slave-gladiator being put to the sword and watched by an indifferent Christian audience from the comfort of good seats in the stands. He wrote, "I think that God has exhibited us apostles as last of all, like men sentenced to death . . . a spectacle to the world."[18]

Soon afterward some rival missionaries arrived in Corinth proclaiming their superiority to Paul and his inferiority to them. Paul responds twice to this triumphalism in 2 Corinthians. In chapter two he casts himself in an anti-triumphalist way:

> But thanks be to God, who in Christ always leads us in triumphal procession, and through us spreads the fragrance of the knowledge of him everywhere. For we are the aroma of Christ to God among those who are being saved and among those who are perishing, to

---

18. 1 Cor 4:9.

one a fragrance from death to death, to the other a fragrance from life to life.[19]

God is leading Paul around like a prisoner of war in a Roman military parade on his way to execution but who nevertheless makes God known wherever he goes. This is Paul's response to the "super-apostles" and their supporters in Corinth, who see him as a perpetually defeated minister.

Later Paul wrote his "Fool's Speech" in which he ironically catalogues his sufferings in the course of preaching the gospel.[20] He actually boasts of suffering incurred as a missionary of Jesus, thereby exposing the superficiality of the "super-apostles."

We may speculate that Paul developed his careful anti-triumphalism as a result of his exposure to the crass triumphalism of Roman cities like *Colonia Caesarea Antiocheia*.

Triumphalism was dominant in the cultures traversed by Paul, whether reflected in the conscious religious superiority of the Pharisees or the self-confident political superiority of the Romans. Based on the humility of Jesus' incarnation and his sacrifice of the cross, Paul diametrically redefined greatness as the service of others, including the weak. It can also be claimed that Paul's anti-triumphalism changed one of the key values of Greco-Roman society. Back then boasting was expected but today it is unacceptable.

Reflection

It wasn't that Paul set out to be a social critic. Rather, Paul identified himself as "a man in Christ," that is, "in Christ *crucified*." For Paul, therefore, legalism was a denial of the grace of God, libertinism an expression of "me-first" selfishness, and elitism and triumphalism embodiments of arrogant superiority.

---

19. 2 Cor 2:14–16.
20. 2 Cor 11:1—13:13.

Fifteen

Problems with Paul

THIS SMALL BOOK IS not a "life of Paul," nor is it a "theology of Paul," nor again is it a combination of both. Rather, it seeks to tell Paul's story and to open windows that reveal Paul's true character, based on his letters. These letters expose Paul's thinking across a considerable span of his career, beginning with Galatians written in AD 48 through to 2 Timothy written in AD 65.[1]

Among the many problems people have with Paul there are four that are prominent. The first is that his words occasionally grate, for example, when he writes, "I am not aware of anything against me" and "be imitators of me."[2] We wonder, "Who does he think he is?"

A second is his teaching on homosexuality and the third is his requirement that wives should "submit" to their husbands. These are critical issues in a modern (western) culture that insists on gender equality.

A fourth problem with Paul is the complaint going back many years that Paul hijacked the teachings of Jesus and took Christianity to intellectual places never intended by its founder.

Paul's Language

Paul's language sometimes sounds arrogant and domineering. But is it?

---

1. Many think Galatians was written in the mid-50s but most would locate Philippians in the early 60s.
2. 1 Cor 4:4, 1.

Statements like "I am not aware of anything against me"[3] prove not to be an issue when we read them in context. Paul was only saying that the Lord, not people, will judge his servants at the end. Meanwhile, it would be inappropriate for the Corinthians, or even Paul himself, to pass judgement on his ministry. Paul was not claiming to be perfect but was only saying that this was not yet the time to judge ministers and their ministries.

It is readily agreed that Paul often comes across as blunt. But it is good to remember that he had spent many years training as a Pharisee. We have only to read the judgments of the rabbis of that era in the *Mishnah* to understand how direct and authoritarian they sound to our ears. Often they speak in an argumentative way to other rabbis. There is a modern parallel in the way lawyers and judges sometimes address one another in court. While Paul had left his Pharisee past behind him after the Damascus "call" we should not be surprised that some of its vestiges should cling to him.

It is also acknowledged that he occasionally sounds rather paternalistic. This is because many of his readers in the churches had only become believers through his ministry. He was their spiritual father. Many times Paul refers to himself as their father and to them as his spiritual children.[4] This helps explain why he comes across to educated people in modern sophisticated societies as rather paternalistic.

Paul was conscious that he had been "called" by Christ to be his ambassador, so that he spoke and wrote with the authority of the one who sent him. This is how we understand the meaning of "apostle" (which means, "sent one"). Its background was in the Jewish practice in that era. The high priest in Jerusalem would send an authorized messenger (a *shaliach*, which in Hebrew also means, "sent one") with *his* decrees to synagogues around the world.

The apostle came with the authority of the sender. Paul was a messenger with the authority of Christ the Divine Sender. Inevitably there is an authoritative tone in Paul's letters. He was an "apostle" of the resurrected Lord.

Paul's words are less likely to annoy us when we understand that he was an ex-Pharisee who, through his ministry, had become a father to the people in the churches, which he did as an apostle of Christ.

---

3. 1 Cor 4:4.

4. For example, "I appeal to you for my child, Onesimus, whose father I became" (Phlm 10).

Speaking personally, I would like my words as examined in later years (a remote possibility!) to be read in the social context in which they were written. We should read Paul's words, written so many years ago, in the same sympathetic spirit.

Paul suffers the undeserved reputation that he was a rather aloof, uncaring person. Even a cursory reading of his letters reveals Paul to have been a sensitive and loving man. Several examples establish this. He pleaded with Philemon to receive back as "a beloved brother" the runaway slave Onesimus, whom he refers to as "my very heart" (Phlm 16, 12). In writing to the Christians in Philippi he was sensitive to their disappointment that Timothy will not be coming to them immediately, but also to the need to shield Epaphroditus from possible criticism over his failed mission in Rome (Phil 2:19–30). These and other examples of his caring leadership help explain the tears of the Ephesian leaders as they farewelled him for the last time (Acts 20:37).

Paul and Homosexuality

There is probably no teaching of Paul's that attracts greater condemnation than his stance on homosexual practice.

While this has been a source of criticism since the days of the Enlightenment, that criticism has become strident since the mid-twentieth century. This is because in opposing homosexuality he was at the same time condemning same-sex marriage. A majority of citizens in most countries strongly support the legal recognition of same-sex marriages.

The problem for Paul is that Jesus is silent on the subject. Jesus commends life-long heterosexual marriage (Mark 10:6–9), but says nothing about homosexuality. Once again, Jesus is seen as good and Paul as bad. Worse for Paul is that apart from his letters, the only other New Testament text is Jude 7, which cites the case of God's punishment on Sodom and Gomorrah.

This isolates Paul as obsessive about homosexuality and invites the suggestion that he struggled with his own sexual demons. Surely his *cri de coeur*, "wretched man that I am," points in that direction (Rom 7:24). Against that, however, Paul only refers to homosexual practice in three of his thirteen letters. While each is a powerful statement, they hardly allow us to typecast him as preoccupied with the homoerotic union. He has far more to say across his letters about loveless and arrogant behavior that divides congregations.

So what does Paul teach? His explanation for homosexual behavior is found near the beginning of the Letter to the Romans.

> For this reason God gave them up to dishonorable passions. For their women exchanged natural relations for those that are contrary to nature; and the men likewise gave up natural relations with women and were consumed with passion for one another, men committing shameless acts with men and receiving in themselves the due penalty for their error.[5]

Paul had just stated that because humanity has rejected the worship of the Creator, preferring to worship the creation, God has "handed them over" to their idolatry and its accompaniment, sexual practices that are "dishonorable," "shameless," and "contrary to nature." In other words, Paul taught that same-sex practices are not what God originally intended and are evidence that humanity has rejected its Creator in favor of idolatry.

His second statement is found in the vice list in 1 Corinthians.

> Or do you not know that the unrighteous will not inherit the kingdom of God? Do not be deceived: neither the sexually immoral, nor idolaters, nor adulterers, nor men who practice homosexuality, nor thieves, nor the greedy, nor drunkards, nor revilers, nor swindlers will inherit the kingdom of God.
>
> And such were some of you.
> > But you were washed,
> > you were sanctified,
> > you were justified
> > > in the name of the Lord Jesus Christ
> > > and by the Spirit of our God.[6]

The seriousness of the vice list is seen in references to "not inherit the kingdom of God" that "bookend" his statement. At the same time, he notes that "some" of the Corinthians, whose lifestyle had been one of vice, have now been delivered from those practices, perhaps including homosexuals.

Included in his list are those Paul calls *malakoi* (literally meaning "soft," referring to passive male partners in the sex act) and the *arsenokoitai*

---

5. Rom 1:26–27.
6. 1 Cor 6:9–11.

(a word combining "male" and "bed" and pointing to active male partners). Paul's words *malakoi* and *arsenokoitai* imply the *act* of sodomy. Paul is not referring to inclination but to actual acts.

Paul's second word, *arsenokoitai*, is a compound of "male" (*arsen*) and "intercourse" (*koitēs*, literally "bed"), words used in the Greek translation of the Leviticus texts suggesting that Paul is linking back to those two passages.

> You shall not lie with (*koitēn*) a male (*arsenos*) as with a woman; it is an abomination.[7]

> If a man lies with a male (*arsenos koitēn*) as with a woman, both of them have committed an abomination; they shall surely be put to death; their blood is upon them.[8]

Leviticus addressed the redeemed people, Israel, who had left behind practices that were rife in Egypt. Paul is addressing his redeemed readers urging them to leave behind practices that were common in the Greco-Roman world.

The third passage is found in Paul's first letter to Timothy.

> Now we know that the law is good, if one uses it lawfully, understanding this, that the law is not laid down for the just but for the lawless and disobedient, for the ungodly and sinners, for the unholy and profane, for those who strike their fathers and mothers, for murderers, the sexually immoral, men who practice homosexuality, enslavers, liars, perjurers, and whatever else is contrary to sound doctrine, in accordance with the gospel of the glory of the blessed God with which I have been entrusted.[9]

"Men who practice homosexuality" is one word in the original text, which is the same that appears in 1 Cor 6:9–11, *arsenokoitai*. Paul is listing various vices as defined by the Law of Moses. Those who accept the gospel of God are expected also to obey the (moral) law of God, as articulated by Moses and the prophets.

So was Paul obsessive regarding homoerotic practice, reflecting perhaps his own suppressed sexual urges? For several reasons this is unlikely.

---

7. Lev 18:22.
8. Lev 20:13.
9. 1 Tim 1:8–11.

For a start, as noted, Paul only addresses the subject in three of his thirteen letters. If the matter were a priority for Paul he would have taught about it in a majority of his letters.

Furthermore, Paul is merely teaching a message that reflected the broader teaching of the Bible on sexuality. In the creation narrative in Gen 1 the injunction "multiply" appears repeatedly. God blessed his animals of sea, land, and air, calling upon them to multiply. In the climax of the narrative God blessed "man in his image," that is "male and female," to "be fruitful and multiply and fill the earth." In other words, God created sex in animals and humans for the procreation of their respective kinds. For animals the exercise of sex is an instinct, but for humans God made it a pleasurable activity. The polarities of male and female in animals and humans, expressed sexually, therefore, are God's provision for the future survival and growth of the respective created species. Paul's rejection of same-sex activity is merely to articulate the biblical tradition established from the beginning.

Josephus, the apologist for Judaism in the era of early Christianity, articulated Jewish views of the era:

> The Law recognizes no sexual connexions, except the natural union of a man and wife, and that only for the procreation of children. Sodomy it abhors, and punishes any guilty of such assault with death. . . . The husband must have union with the wife alone . . . The Law orders all the offspring to be brought up, and forbids women either to cause abortion or to make away with the foetus.[10]

Neither Jesus nor Paul sanctioned violence against sexual offenders. We recall Jesus preventing the stoning of the woman caught in the act of adultery. Paul taught that the unrepentant faced exclusion from the kingdom of God.

Nevertheless, the evidence points to both holding firm, covenant-based attitudes toward stable marriages as the setting for begetting and raising children. We should be confident that Paul's master, Jesus, would have held the same views. Jesus did not articulate an opinion on homosexuality in the Gospels because there was no need to. God's covenant people had long since confirmed the importance of family life based on heterosexual relationships between a husband and a wife.

---

10. Josephus, *Against Apion* 2. 199–202.

Again, Paul's was not the only voice from antiquity that rejected homosexual practice. The Greeks regarded heterosexual relationships as "natural" and homosexual acts as "unnatural." Aristotle observed that "the affection between a man and a woman . . . happen according to nature."[11]

This recognition, however, which was widespread, proved to be no barrier to widespread homosexual practice among the Greeks and Romans.[12] This was Paul's point throughout his letters, especially in Romans. Gentiles and Jews have their standards, but do not live up to them.

Same-sex activity was common in antiquity. It was part of the behavior of the Egyptians from whom the Israelites had come as it was also of the Canaanites to whom they were going.[13] Such practices were commonplace in the lands around the Mediterranean visited by Paul that had been subject to Greek influence and to Roman conquest. Julius Caesar was a known bisexual who was said to be "every woman's man and every man's woman."[14] The emperor Nero had a boy named Sporus castrated, "married" him with all ceremony, and lived with him as a wife.

Paul's Teaching on Man-Woman Relationships

Paul is criticized, even vilified, for his teaching on man-woman relationships. He is often called a misogynist and his teachings on the subject labelled as oppressive.

While those teachings are confined to 1 Corinthians, Ephesians, Colossians, and his first letter to Timothy, nevertheless they were part of the tradition he gave to each church at the time of its foundation. In other words, his teachings on the subject were universally given to his network of mission churches.[15]

There are several critical elements of Paul's teachings on this subject. Paul insisted that gender distinctions between males and females are to be maintained. Men were to look like men and women were to look like women. In that culture it meant that men were to have short hair and women long hair. Paul regarded the gender distinctions as God-given.

11. *Nichomachean Ethics* 1162a.
12. For a study of Greek attitudes toward sexual practices, including homosexuality, see Thornton, *Eros*.
13. Lev 18:1–3, 22; 29:13.
14. Suetonius, *Julius Caesar* 1.52.3.
15. 1 Cor 11:2, 16.

Consistently, husbands and wives were to have differing and complementary roles. Paul based relationships between a husband and wife on the analogy of Christ and the church. Christ is the "head" of his "body," the church.[16] Christ the head loved his body the church and sacrificed himself for her. Likewise, husbands are sacrificially to love their wives and wives are to submit to their husbands, as the church submits to Christ. The verb *hypotassomai*, translated "submit to," literally means "rank oneself under," which metaphorically means, "to respect," "to look up to." It means to recognize and respect a husband's God-given role in the marriage and the family.

A wife's acknowledgement of the headship of her husband was to be expressed outwardly by her appearance. In that culture a married woman wore her hair in a particularly tidy arrangement. Paul insisted that a wife observed that convention when she exercised charismatic gifts like prophesying and praying. Not to do so would be to deny the authority of her husband and to demean him publicly.

At the same time, Paul teaches *interdependence* between husband and wife.

> In the Lord woman is not independent of man nor man of woman.[17]

> The husband should give to his wife her conjugal rights, and likewise the wife to her husband. For the wife does not have authority over her own body, but the husband does. Likewise the husband does not have authority over his own body, but the wife does.[18]

We may think that Paul's words about a husband's headship were due to the widespread female illiteracy in that era. However, numbers of women in Paul's mission were socially prominent (which then meant educated), for example, Priscilla, Chloe, Phoebe, Lydia, Euodia, and Syntyche. Paul could have made an exception for them as mission leaders but does not do so. Indeed, it is possible that due to their high social status and missionary prominence that some of them believed these differentiating conventions did not apply to them.

Given the current insistence on gender equality in western culture, these explanations of Paul's teaching will scarcely prove acceptable. Let me offer several further comments.

16. Eph 5:22–33.
17. 1 Cor 11:11.
18. 1 Cor 7:3.

Paul took very seriously the divinely given order in the early chapters of Genesis. On the one hand Eve was created from Adam, but on the other there was complementarity and interdependence.[19] In other words, Paul's views were consistent with the Bible's narrative in its foundation chapters.

Although the Gospels are silent on Jesus' views on spousal relationships, it is all but certain that Paul believed his teachings were consistent with those of the Lord. Paul, the servant of Jesus, would not have deliberately gone in a different direction to his Lord on such an important matter. Paul was not the only apostle to teach that a wife is to be subject to her husband. Peter, who had been a disciple of Jesus, also teaches this.[20] We are right to assume the apostles' man-woman teachings were in line with the teachings of Jesus.

Significantly, Paul broke with Jewish practice that only husbands could initiate divorce. Paul gives to a wife the right to separate from her husband.[21] This represented a massive and liberating social change.

It is important that Paul addresses husbands and wives separately, calling on them voluntarily to fulfill their distinctive responsibilities. Paul calls on the husbands to love their wives as Christ loved the church. In Eph 5:22-33 Paul repeatedly instructs husbands to love their wives, that is, sacrificially.

It is not up to a wife to impose that duty on her husband. It is not up to a husband to impose a duty on his wife to submit to him. Paul calls on each partner voluntarily to fulfill his or her God-given role as "unto the Lord." For both, it is not a cold duty but an expression of love and obedience to Jesus. The wife is not to demand love from her husband and the husband is not to demand submission (respect) from his wife. Each is first to respond separately to the Lord.

Paul's particular emphasis is on husbands loving and cherishing their wives. Thus understood there is absolutely no place for a husband's coercion, manipulation, or abusive behavior.

Paul's teaching implies that the "office" of the man is to provide for, protect, and care for his wife and his children, and moreover to take responsibility in partnership with his wife for the spiritual wellbeing of the family.

---

19. Gen 2:24.
20. 1 Pet 3:1.
21. 1 Cor 7:10.

Paul leaves the actual outworking of spousal relationships undefined and open. This means that couples will work things out according to their circumstances, including a wife's involvement in the workforce. Also, they will reach a working consensus about who does what in the family. For example, some wives manage the family finances and pay the bills.

It should also be noted that health issues frequently change the dynamics of husband-wife relationships, for example, where the husband becomes ill. Should the tragedy of Alzheimer's disease strike down a husband, then the wife must assume sole leadership for him and her. In other words, the spousal roles as outlined by Paul are not absolute but relative and subject to change.

Having explained and defended Paul's views it will still be difficult in the extreme for many to appreciate them, much less fall in with them. Our modern world is steeped in the ideal of equality and that the roles of male and female are interchangeable.

Still, it is worth pondering that the fundamental differences between men and women remain, which the feminist revolution has not removed. Could it be that, when Paul's teachings are sympathetically applied by both husband and wife they are actually found to work to the enrichment of both men and women and the children born to their care?

The Proposal that Paul Was the Real Founder of Christianity

Famous playwright George Bernard Shaw blamed Paul for turning Christianity into "Crosstianity," a teaching focused on the crucifixion of Jesus for the forgiveness of sins. Paul claimed to have "the mind of Christ"[22] but according to Shaw and others that was far from the truth.

William Wrede even referred to Paul as "the second founder of Christianity . . . and not for the better."[23] This view was made popular in Nikos Kazantzakis' book, *The Last Temptation of Christ* (1955), which Martin Scorcese made into a movie of that name (1988).

Today there are many who regard Jesus positively but who reject Paul. Like Shaw, Wrede, and Kazantzakis, they believe that Paul took the teaching of Jesus in directions that he never intended. They object most strongly to Paul's teachings about the crucifixion as the divine source of forgiveness.

22. 1 Cor 2:16.
23. Wrede, *Paul*, 148, 151.

This is an objection that is not difficult to correct. Twice in Paul's first letter to the Corinthians, written AD 55, Paul quotes preformulated teachings that go back to the period immediately after Jesus. One such tradition repeats exactly the words of Jesus at the Last Supper, the other to the facts of Jesus' death, burial, resurrection, and resurrection appearances. The Last Supper tradition states that the body of Jesus was given "*for* you" and the Easter tradition that the "Christ died *for* our sins."

In other words, Paul did not invent the death of Christ as atoning for sins. Rather, he merely passed on a teaching that went back to Jesus and the earliest church. Those two preformatted traditions decisively overturn the idea that Paul invented the atonement theology. It was already there in the mind of Jesus and the original disciples.

This theory imagines that Paul willfully set out to change Jesus' message. However, Paul the newly converted Pharisee spent fifteen days in the house of Peter and also visited James the Lord's brother.[24] He visited Jerusalem subsequently when his theological teaching was scrutinized and approved by the apostles.[25]

If there was a founder of Christianity, apart from Jesus, then all fingers must point to Peter. Peter was the first to address Jesus as the Christ, and the first to preach Jesus as the Christ. If we are thinking about a subsidiary founder of Christianity, that honor must be given to the one Jesus called Cephas, "Rock."

Rather than Paul having invented these teachings the evidence points to Paul as a faithful teacher of doctrines that actually arose from Jesus. It seems, rather, that Shaw and others simply disliked this teaching and for that reason sought to discredit it.

Reflection

I think it is possible to explain and defend Paul's teachings that have proved controversial. If his language come across as authoritarian or paternalistic the reasons for this are not hard to find. Paul had been a Pharisee who became an apostle of Christ and the "father" of those to whom he wrote.

Contrary to the views of many Paul was not obsessed with homosexuality. His views on marriage and sexuality merely express the long-held understanding of God's covenant with his people going back to early

---

24. Gal 1:18–20.
25. Gal 2:1–9.

Genesis, views that Jesus also would have upheld. Moreover, Paul mentions homosexual practice in only three of his thirteen letters. It was widely believed that homosexuality was contrary to nature, although its practice was common.

Paul taught about husband-wife relationships from the perspective of the early chapters of Genesis and did so in a social setting where some wives were rejecting the cultural signs of their marriage. Paul was concerned for the stability of marriages in his mission network and for male and female partners to fulfill their distinctive roles in relationship with one another.

The view that Paul invented the doctrines of atonement based on his own willful decisions simply does not stand up to scrutiny.

Paul has been and will remain a controversial figure, but when his teachings are examined they prove to be edifying and helpful.

Sixteen

Three Questions about Paul

OF THE MANY QUESTIONS about Paul there are three of significant importance. The first is: why does Paul say so little about Jesus the figure of history? Was it that he didn't know, or for that matter, didn't care? Or, was there another reason? The second question relates to the second coming of Jesus. Paul believed that Jesus would return, but was it immediately or was it over the horizon? A third question is: did Paul believe his letters were Scripture?

Why Doesn't Paul Say More about Jesus of Nazareth?

Paul's letters are our earliest window into Christian beliefs in the first generation after Jesus. The Gospels belong to the next generation and are dependent on preexisting oral and written sources that go back to Jesus.

29–33	Jesus
34–65	Paul
65–80	Gospels

Paul's letters contain snippets of information about the historical figure of Jesus. In 1 Corinthians, for example, we catch a glimpse of Jesus at the Last Supper, the betrayal of Jesus, his crucifixion, and his resurrection. We hear his words about marriage and the payment of ministers.

When we examine Paul's other letters we find references to James, brother of Jesus, to twelve disciples led by Peter, and to Pontius Pilate.

Compared to the mass of detail in the Gospels, however, the historical information about Jesus in Paul's letters is not extensive.

It's not that Paul didn't know about Jesus. Three years after the Damascus encounter he returned to Jerusalem where he had extensive meetings with Peter, with other original disciples of Jesus, and with James the brother of the Lord.[1] In other words, although so far as we know Paul had not met Jesus, he had met his brother (possibly also his mother) and had come to know those who had been with Jesus throughout the years of his ministry.

When Paul established churches in distant places we can be confident that the new converts had many questions about Jesus. How old was he? What was his background? What had he done in Galilee and Judea? Why was he killed? Who witnessed his resurrection?

Paul's church members already knew the answers to these and other historical questions about Jesus because he had already told them. Paul wrote his letters to address other and more current issues. For example, the Galatian Christians needed to know whether it was necessary for non-Jews to adopt Jewish practices. Likewise the Corinthians needed to know that "all things" (including promiscuous behavior) were not lawful as they were assuming them to be.

Paul's relative silence about the historical Jesus does not mean that his letters lacked a narrative about him. There is, in fact, a powerful strand of teaching about Jesus that runs throughout Paul's letters, but it is one that transcends mere historical information.

In Galatians, probably Paul's earliest letter, he wrote, "When the fullness of time had come, God sent forth his Son . . . to redeem those who were under the law."[2] In 1 Corinthians, written midway through Paul's span of letter writing, he stated that "all things" (in creation and redemption) "are through" the "one Lord, Jesus Christ."[3] Finally, in Philippians, one of Paul's last letters, he wrote that Jesus had been "in the form of God," having "equality with God," but voluntarily took "the form of a servant" who endured "death on a cross" but whom God "highly exalted" and at "whose name every knee should bow."[4]

No doubt Paul was mindful of Jesus' wonderful example as teacher, healer and friend, which we read about in the Gospels. But these are not the

---

1. Gal 1:18–19.
2. Gal 4:4.
3. 1 Cor 8:6.
4. Phil 2:5–11.

actions of Jesus that Paul wanted to bring before his readers. Rather, Paul widens his angle to let them see Jesus from eternity to eternity, as preexistent, incarnate, exalted, and returning. Jesus was the one, who though rich became poor to make the poor rich.[5]

Jesus preexistent >| Jesus incarnate >| Jesus resurrected and returning

This was Paul's narrative about the *transcendent* Son of God that runs through his letters from first to last.

Of course, the original disciples shared the same view of Jesus, but it came to them by a process that was different from Paul's. The twelve first encountered Jesus as a rabbi and prophet and only gradually came to recognize his divinity and finally only fully at his resurrection.

On the other hand, Jesus himself confronted Paul as "Lord" outside Damascus. Paul only later came to know about his historical deeds through contact with Peter, James, and the disciples in Jerusalem. We can understand, therefore, that Paul's letters place greater emphasis on the transcendent Jesus and less on the historical Jesus. Similarly, we understand why the Gospels, which arose from the witness of the original disciples, portray them struggling to understand Jesus' identity before grasping that he was the Lord.

At Damascus God revealed to Paul that Jesus the Son of God preexisted history, intersected history, and overarched history from creation to new creation. That narrative runs like a golden thread through Paul's preaching and letters from first to last.

Did Paul Preach the Immediate Return of Jesus?

It is popularly but incorrectly believed that Paul preached the *immediate* return of Jesus.

Rather, Paul's letters suggest that he expected Jesus to return during his lifetime. That seems clear from his words to the Thessalonians ("*we* who are alive, who are left until the coming of the Lord") and to the Corinthians ("*we* will not all die, but *we* will all be changed").[6] The Thessalonians "turned to God from idols to *wait* for his Son from heaven."[7]

---

5. 2 Cor 8:9.
6. 1 Thess 4:15; 1 Cor 15:51.
7. 1 Thess 1:9–10.

The expectation of the return of the Lord depended on the fact of his resurrection from the dead. Jesus' resurrection marked the beginning of the Great Resurrection, which in turn signalled the absolute end of history.[8] In that vein he wrote to the Romans that "the night is far gone, the day is at hand. So then let us cast off the works of darkness and put on the armor of light."[9]

Because of the resurrection of Jesus, Paul believed that "the end of the ages" had come upon his generation,[10] that it was now the beginning of the "last days," "the beginning of the end." Nevertheless, certain events must first take place, for example, what Paul mysteriously calls "the rebellion" when the "man of lawlessness," the "son of destruction is revealed."[11] The return of Jesus would not occur without these prior events.

It is clear that Paul thought the return of the Lord was sufficiently distant for him to plan an ambitious missionary journey being launched from Rome to Spain.

Paul's expectation of the return of Jesus was a major motivation for his ministry. But it must be remembered that what God had done in the past in raising Jesus from the dead was *the* event upon which the future depended. So far as Paul was concerned the center of all things was not so much in the future as in *the past* because of what God had *already* done in Christ's atoning death and hope-giving resurrection.

Paul believed that the last phase of history had begun but he still planned future missionary work in distant lands.

Paul's example is worth noting. He believed that Jesus' return was within his lifetime while still making significant plans for missionary service into the indefinite future. His conviction about the return of the Lord did not freeze his missionary activism but rather energized it.

Did Paul Regard His Letters as Scripture?

The answer is, yes he did.

The critical detail is that Paul wrote his letters very carefully with the specific intention that they were to be read aloud in church meetings. Not

---

8. 1 Cor 15:20, 23.
9. Rom 15:12.
10. 1 Cor 10:11.
11. 2 Thess 2:3.

only so, but that churches were to copy his texts and exchange them with other churches.

> When this letter has been read among you, have it read in the church of the Laodiceans: and see that you also read the letter from Laodicea.[12]

As a rabbi, Paul was used to the reading of the Law, the prophets, and the writings being read and applied in the synagogues. There were many other Jewish writings from that era but only those that were officially regarded as Scripture were read in the public assembly of the people of God. Paul wrote texts to be read in the churches. This indicates his belief that his written words carried canonical status, and were on par with the writings of the Old Testament.

Consistent with this is his comment to the Corinthians:

> If any one thinks he is a prophet, or spiritual, he should acknowledge that the things I am *writing* to you are a *command* of the Lord.[13]

Paul's written words, he said, bear the authority of the risen and ascended Lord.

In similar vein, he informed the Corinthians of "the *authority* that the Lord has given me for building you up."[14]

Paul, as an ambassador of Christ, was his surrogate whose command was *as if* from the Lord himself. In other words, Paul saw himself as bearing the authority of the Lord as Moses saw himself bearing the authority of the Lord Almighty.

Peter referred to Paul's letters as "Scripture."[15] The early church of the following centuries included Paul's letters in the canon of the New Testament.

Conclusion

Paul knew about Jesus through his extensive relationship with James, brother of the Lord, on the one hand, and with Peter and other disciples of

---

12. Col 4:17.
13. 1 Cor 14:37.
14. 2 Cor 10:8; 13:10.
15. 2 Pet 3:15–17.

Jesus on the other. There are two main reasons Paul did not have more to say about Jesus of Nazareth in his letters. The first was that Paul would have supplied this information when he established the churches. Paul wrote his letters because the receiving churches were facing serious theological or moral challenges. Paul's initial encounter with Jesus was as the transcendent Lord and only later was he able to fill in the blanks about Jesus the man. For Paul his abiding awareness of Jesus was from the Damascus encounter.

Paul was convinced that Jesus would return before he died, although he knew of a number of events that must come first. Paul was energized by his conviction of the Lord's return, but he was not paralyzed into inaction by the belief that the return was to occur immediately, the next day.

Paul wrote with the authority of the risen Lord, and Peter and the early church regarded his writings as Scripture.

Seventeen

A New Perspective on Paul?

PEOPLE FROM THE ERA of the New Testament were deeply conscious of the ethnic and cultural divisions within the human race. Greeks regarded non-Greeks as "barbarians," uncivilized and uneducated. The Romans also employed that term for the wild Germanic and other tribes who lived outside their northern boundaries, and who were a constant threat. Jews were deeply aware of their identity as God's chosen people, regarding all others as "gentiles," people of the "nations."

Along with the sense of division there was also the sense of superiority. Greeks and Romans knew they were superior to Barbarians just as Jews knew they were superior to gentiles.

Paul had two reasons to feel superior: he was a Jew and he was a Roman citizen. God's "call" to Paul outside Damascus changed everything, as he informed the Roman readers:

> I am under obligation both to *Greeks* and to *barbarians*.... The gospel ... is the power of God for salvation to everyone who believes, to the *Jew* first and also to the *Greek* [i.e., gentile].[1]

He explains why he felt obligated to *all* ethnic groups:

> For we hold that one is justified by faith apart from works of the law. Or is God the God of *Jews* only? Is he not the God of *gentiles* also? Yes, of gentiles also, since God is one—who will justify *the circumcised* by faith and *the uncircumcised* through faith.[2]

1. Rom 1:14, 16.
2. Rom 3:28–30.

God is "one" and is the God of all people, Jews and gentiles. Consistently, God has one and only one way of putting people from both ethnicities in a right relationship with him. He justifies Jews by faith, and he justifies gentiles through faith.[3]

Inextricably connected with one message to both Jews and gentiles was Paul's insistence on the social unity of mixed congregations.

> For as many of you as were baptized into Christ have put on Christ. There is neither Jew nor Greek, there is neither slave nor free, there is no male and female, for you are all one in Christ Jesus.[4]

At that time the great barrier to ethnic unity was the Jews' refusal to share a meal with gentiles. Paul vigorously opposed the refusal of Christian Jews in Antioch to eat with gentile believers.[5] He devised pastoral advice to assist both groups finding a practical way of eating together: the gentiles were to eat only what was acceptable with the Jews.[6] The strong were to accommodate to the scruples of the weak.

Paul's application of the same message about Jesus to both Jews and gentiles—in effect to all humanity—makes him a genuine and inclusive humanist, whose voice speaks to us from distant Greco-Roman antiquity.

A New Perspective

Some years ago another view about Paul became current, particularly associated with distinguished scholars Krister Stendahl, E. P. Sanders, and James Dunn. It stated that God's covenant with the Jewish race remained intact, and was only inapplicable where Jews repudiated it. Unless a Jew opted out he or she remained in the covenant.

According to this opinion, Paul developed a special provision for gentiles to be included in the covenant with Jews, which was by faith in Christ and baptism. A gentile's faith in Christ attracted the divine approval. He or she was thereby justified, justified *by faith*.

The new perspective correctly states that the Lord freely chose Israel, freely delivered her from slavery in Egypt, freely gave her his law, and freely

---

3. No significance is inferred by the literary variation "by" and "through."
4. Gal 3:27–28.
5. Gal 2:11–14.
6. Rom 14:1—15:7.

A New Perspective on Paul?

brought her into the promised land. Israel's response to the Lord was to remain faithful to the Law given to Moses at Mt. Sinai.

Israel was thus in the covenant with God and her members only ceased to be if they chose not to be, or had committed heinous sin. The coming of Christ did not affect Israel's Law-based covenant with God. It remained current and effective.

Israel tacitly confirmed her covenantal relationship with the Lord by observing the "works of the law"—male circumcision, observance of the Sabbath and the feasts, and the dietary and purity rules. These works served to separate the holy nation from the nations of the world, the gentiles.

The new perspective does not regard these works as attracting merit from God. Rather they are like traffic rules, observed as routine and not accruing credit with the Almighty. God's grace initiated the covenant and that grace sustains it for God's chosen people.

The coming of Christ and the apostolic preaching of the gospel did not affect Israel's covenantal relationship with God. Israel was in the covenant and her continuing response was to stay in and not choose to leave, or commit serious sin.

Accordingly, Paul's teaching about "justification by faith" was in no way directed to Jews, but was only directed to and for the gentiles. Gentiles were justified by faith when they exercised faith in Christ and were baptized in his name.

In effect, then, there were two parallel covenants, one for the historic people of God, the other for the people of the nations.

This new perspective on Paul has proved attractive and has many supporters.

Problems with the New Perspective on Paul

There are, however, a number of problems. The first is that the Lord's covenant with his people was not, in fact, intact but broken. The narratives of the books of Samuel and Kings are catalogues of the failure of kings and people to observe the laws that God had revealed at Mt Sinai. In every epoch—Assyrian, Babylonian, Persian, Greek—the Lord's prophets condemned the people for failure to uphold the revealed will of God. Jeremiah declared the existing covenant irreparably broken, promising a *"new covenant* with the house of Israel and the house of Judah."[7]

7. Jer 31:31–34.

Jesus, aware of Jeremiah's words, declared that his death had inaugurated a *new* covenant.[8] The apostle Paul stated that he was a "minister of the *new* covenant."[9] In other words, the Lord and the apostle to the gentiles disaffirmed the currency of the former covenant.

Secondly, Paul taught that it is only by faith that gentiles *and* Jews are "justified," i.e., by God. When Peter came to Antioch he insisted that Jewish believers separate from their gentile brethren at meals.[10] Paul, however, pointed out that demanding gentiles obey the works of the law (dietary rules) was to deny the "truth of the gospel." He and Peter, although Jews and not sin-practicing gentiles, were absolutely dependent on God to be justified by faith, and not by works of the law.[11] If Jews like them were justified by faith, then so too were gentiles. Because neither group was obligated to observe works of the law, therefore both were equally free from the necessity to comply with a dietary code.

Paul taught that works of the law were the tangible expressions of the law, not merely social markers differentiating Jews from gentiles. "Law" was as incapable as "works of the law" to bring divine justification, as Paul informed the Galatian Christians:

Galatians

3:11   Now it is evident that no one is justified before God by the law, for "the righteous shall live by faith."

5:3–4 I testify again to every man who accepts circumcision that he is obligated to keep the whole law.
You are severed from Christ, you who would be justified by the law; you have fallen away from grace.

The new perspective distinguishes works of the law from the Law. Paul, however, regards works of the Law as the practical expression of what it means to be subject to the Law.[12]

We ask the question: which did Paul see as more fundamental in a relationship with God, the Law or faith? For Paul, faith was the divine priority. Abrahams's faith in God's promise preceded the giving of the Law by

---

8. Luke 22:20; 1 Cor 11:25.
9. 2 Cor 3:6.
10. Gal 2:11–13.
11. Gal 2:11–16.
12. E.g., "Tell me, you who desire to be under the law" (Gal 4:21).

A New Perspective on Paul?

many centuries.[13] It was by that man's faith in God that he was deemed righteous.[14] Furthermore, Law had only a temporary role in the Old Testament narrative "until Christ came,"[15] but faith had always been the appropriate response to God's promises.

Paul spent much of his time pleading with Jews to accept the priority of faith in Christ over works of the Law. The pursuit of righteousness via the Law must end in failure, he said, but the way of faith in Christ issued in divine acceptance and approval.[16]

There is at least one other problem with the new perspective on Paul, namely its assertion that "works of the Law" did not accrue merit with God, but were practical day-to-day rules, which were merely social in their significance.

It is not difficult, however, to find texts prior to and after the coming of Jesus suggesting that the fulfillment of such works was intended to establish a store of righteousness.

> The beginning of wisdom is the most sincere desire for instruction, and concern for instruction is love of her, and love of her is the keeping of her laws, and giving heed to her laws is *assurance of immortality*, and immortality brings one near to God; so the desire for wisdom leads to a kingdom.[17]

> Whoever honors his father *atones for his sins*, and whoever glorifies his mother is like one who lays up treasure. . . . For kindness to a father *will not be forgotten*, and *against your sins it will be credited*.[18]

The *Mishnah* is a collection of Jewish teachings from about AD 200 but many of those teachings were current in the time of Paul.

> Great is the law, for *it gives life to them that practice it* both in this world and in the world to come.[19]

---

13. Gal 3:17.

14. Gen 15:6—"And he believed the Lord, and it was counted to him as righteousness." See also Rom 4:1–25.

15. Gal 3:25—"The law was our guardian until Christ came."

16. Gal 3:10–11.

17. Wis 6:17–18.

18. *Sirach* 3:3–4, 14.

19. *Aboth* 6:7.

The Holy One, blessed is he, was minded to grant *merit* to Israel; therefore hath he multiplied for them the law and commandments, as it is written, *It pleased the Lord for his righteousness' sake to magnify the law and make it honorable.*[20]

"Life" (i.e., *eternal* life) and "merit" flow from the good works. Clearly this is contrary to the new perspective's assertion that at heart the Law-based covenant was *grace*-based.

Conclusion

God's revelation of his Son to Paul outside Damascus showed him that faith in that Son, and not law-keeping, was the pathway to acceptance with God ("justification"), and regeneration as an adopted child of God. From that time Paul contended that faith in Christ not works of the law was the divine priority.

"The new perspective on Paul" is a misnomer. "Perspective" is a word used by artists, photographers, and architects to describe different angles from which to view a landscape, a person, or a building. The point is that the object is the same and a new perspective is just a different way of seeing it.

The new perspective on Paul, however, does not represent another way of looking at Paul's teaching but represents a *different* teaching altogether. It's not so much a perspective of Paul as a revision of Paul, a rewriting of his theology.

---

20. *Makkot* 3.16.

Eighteen

The Legacy of Paul

WE BEGAN THIS BOOK about Paul by acknowledging his greatness. Then we attempted a short survey of his life from birth to death. In examining Paul's attitude to various people we have been able to see aspects of this man as a leader that many may not have previously noticed. Without delving too much into Paul's theology it was important to reflect on his view of the world, to think about several frequently asked questions, and to be reminded of his concerns about the churches. Aware that Paul has always been a controversial figure we noted problems that some people have with him.

So we come, finally, to think about his legacy. This falls into two parts, matters like his influence on politics, work ethic, and family life on the one hand, and his teachings about Jesus, whose servant he was, on the other. We will consider Paul's ethical influence and then his spiritual influence.

Paul's Ethical Influence

Separating Caesar from God

Under Paul's leadership the new Christian was baptized using the words "Jesus is Lord." This was directly opposite to the creed of the Roman Empire, which was "Caesar is Lord." For Paul, personally, this was an incredible reversal since he was a Roman citizen *by birth*. Caesar, the official title for the emperor, expected absolute loyalty, as if a god. Paul taught that Christ's followers were to give this allegiance to Christ alone. This was radical and potentially dangerous.

At the same time, however, Paul instructed believers to respect the role God gave to Caesar. "Let every person be subject to the governing authorities," he wrote, adding, "Pay what is owed to them: taxes to whom taxes are owed, respect to whom respect is owed, honor to whom honor is owed."[1]

The responsibility of Caesar was the collection of taxes to pay for the administration of society. But Caesar's claims to divinity and worship were to be rejected.

In this Paul was restating a judgment of Jesus. Paul's word "pay" in Greek exactly repeats Jesus' word "render," as in, "Render to Caesar the things that are Caesar's" (that is, "pay the taxes").[2] But Jesus' prior calling was, "Render to God the things that are God's."

"Caesar" was not a personal name but a title for the ruler of the empire. That single word captured the idea of the office of a ruler, as distinct from his identity or moral character. In Jesus' day the actual Caesar was Tiberius, and when Paul wrote Romans the Caesar was Nero, both evil men. Yet Jesus, followed by Paul, taught that the office of rulership was to be respected despite the identities and moral character of the two men.

What is the explanation for this? It is because, on the one hand, anarchy is the worst circumstance for society, and on the other, that even evil rulers generally maintain some semblance of order in society? Hitler was an exception, as his Nazis were actually a group of criminals who were committed to genocide.

In the next centuries the teaching of Jesus as relayed by Paul came to influence important values in society, including the separation of Caesar from God. First, the responsibility to pay taxes and to honor the office of Caesar meant being a responsible, tax-paying member of the community. Another was the right to obey God in matters of personal conscience despite the demands of Caesar to follow his directives. Yet another was the separation of church and state, which is fundamental of liberal democracy.

Jesus' words as Paul reasserted them implicitly reject the notion of theocracy where to obey "Caesar" was to obey God and to obey God was to obey Caesar. Under a theocracy Caesar is the embodiment of divinity. According to Jesus, as followed by Paul, Caesar is to be honored but not worshipped because Caesar is not God.

1. Rom 13:1–7.
2. Mark 12:17; Rom 13:7.

We take human rights for granted, but they were often slow in coming and achieved only after long struggles. These include the accountability of rulers under the same law as others, the right not to be detained by police unless charged, the presumption of innocence until proved guilty in a fair trial, and the right to remain silent when arrested. Some of these rights had antecedents in Roman law but all of them reached their present form in societies influenced by the teaching of Jesus and through the words of his servant, Paul.

This high claim is supported by their failure to emerge in other cultures, for example, from the cultures of the Chinese or the medieval Arabs, both of which were technologically more advanced than Europe or England. The Chinese invented gunpowder and printing before the Europeans and the Arab adaptation of Indian numerals was perhaps the greatest scientific innovation of the first millennium. Yet it was not in China or in Arabian societies but in Christian England that the Magna Carta was promulgated, a king executed for crimes against his people, parliamentary democracy instituted, and the legal rights of individuals great and small secured under the law.

Slavery

The Jews in the time of Jesus kept slaves but the law of God required their liberty after seven years.[3] Slavery under the Jews was less common than among the Greeks and Romans, who had slave-based economies. Jesus did not refer to actual slavery but he condemned the idea of slavery, metaphorically speaking. He said that the Jews who rejected him were slaves to sin and judgement but that he the Son of God would set them free.[4] Because slavery in the metaphor was evil it must mean that Jesus believed that the reality of slavery was evil.

Likewise Paul spoke metaphorically of the "yoke of slavery" and pleaded with his readers to cherish and cling to their freedom.[5] For him slavery as a metaphor was evil and liberty good. Paul also referred to literal slavery. He urged slaves to secure their freedom if they could and in the meantime instructed masters to treat their slaves kindly.[6] He even applied

---

3. Exod 21:2.
4. John 8:31–32.
5. Gal 5:1.
6. 1 Cor 7:21; Eph 6:9.

moral pressure on a Christian slave owner to give a slave his freedom.[7] Clearly Paul, like Jesus, believed slavery was evil and freedom was good.

If we ask why Jesus and Paul were not more direct in calling for the abolition of slavery, the answer is simple. It would be centuries before society was ready to implement that idea. Had slaves sought their liberty en masse at the height of the Roman Empire the slaves would have been crucified in the thousands, as they had been in the slave uprising under Spartacus in the previous century. Mercifully, slavery essentially disappeared in the years after Constantine converted the empire to Christianity.

Tragically, slave trading reemerged in Christian Europe in the eighteenth century, ironically during the Enlightenment, the era that exalted humanity and diminished God. Enlightenment leaders played no great part in the abolition of slave trading. That only occurred through the Herculean efforts over many decades by many, including evangelical Christians led by the parliamentarian William Wilberforce, who was inspired by the converted slave master and church minister John Newton.

Gender, Marriage, and Family

Paul assumed that women would speak prophetically in the church meeting in Corinth.[8] His issue was that some married women were prophesying at church meetings *as if* they were not married. Respectable married women arranged their hair according to cultural convention of the times but these wives were disregarding those practices. They prophesied not as married women, but as if they were men.

In the course of Paul's response he asserted the need for men and women to be identifiably male or female by the length of their hair, which was the means of gender identification at that time. Of course, those conventions change, so Paul is not imposing a permanent rule on hair length. The point, though, is that Paul was following Jesus and the biblical tradition in recognizing the fundamental importance of gender differences.

Gender differences are being blurred in today's post-biblical world. Some refer to themselves as pansexual, others as transgender or even gender-fluid. There are dozens of new gender definitions.

In Paul's day sex between a man and a boy (pederasty) was common and not disapproved, whereas adult male homosexuality was common but

---

7. Phlm 17, 21.
8. 1 Cor 11:2–16.

The Legacy of Paul

frowned upon. In particular, the men who were habitually the passive sexual partners (*kinaidoi*) were despised. Although Greek philosophers, poets, and playwrights mocked and shamed male homosexuality as unnatural, the practice was widespread.[9] Paul went further. He declared that those who engaged in male homosexual acts would not inherit the kingdom of God.[10] This meant that those who practiced sodomy would have been excluded from the membership of the church.

For Paul, the only legitimate expression of sexuality was within heterosexual marriage, based on lifelong, exclusive commitment.[11] All other expressions—incest, pre-marital sex, adultery, bestiality, homosexuality—were regarded as *porneia*, "fornication."

Paul was following Jesus who taught that "from the beginning of creation God made them *male* and *female*," who "shall become *one* flesh," and that "what . . . God *joined together* let not man separate."[12] Jesus' words addressed the issue that was current among the Jews, divorce and remarriage. There are no references in the Gospels, however, to homosexuality because the Jews in Israel at that time did not practise sodomy, or for that matter incest or bestiality.[13]

In the world of the Greeks and Romans to which Paul went, however, various expressions of *porneia* were common. Paul interpreted and adapted his Lord's teachings away from his homeland in Jerusalem into the very different ethos of the Greeks and Romans, where standards and expectations in sexual matters were different.

Paul devoted considerable space in his letters to the family unit. Several times he speaks in turn to husbands, wives, and children.[14] Churches met in the homes of the people. Paul used family words "brother" and "sister" to describe the members, who were to greet each other affectionately at the meetings.

By the time of Paul's missions in the Greek and Roman world, Jewish numbers had multiplied dramatically, mainly through natural biological

---

9. Thornton, *Eros*, 106–20.

10. 1 Cor 6:9–11. The connecting of the words *malakoi* ("soft men," a reference to the passive partners) and *arsenokoitai* ("men who have sex with men," i.e., the active partners) points to male-to-male sexual intercourse.

11. Rom 7:2; 1 Cor 7:2, 39; 1 Thess 4:3–8.

12. Mark 10:6–9.

13. Gagnon, *Bible and Homosexual Practice*, 188–93.

14. Eph 5:22—6:4; Col 3:18–21.

growth reinforced by their refusal to abort their unborn children. Through Paul's missions Christian numbers grew even more dramatically. Like the Jews they rejected the termination of fetuses, but unlike the Jews they engaged in evangelism. Judaism wasn't an active missionary movement, but Pauline Christianity was.

In the following centuries Christianity—in Europe, North Africa, the Middle East, and the Far East—adopted Paul's teachings about gender, sexual practices, and family values. These became the norm in countries of Christian heritage until recent times.

Work

The economies of Greece and Rome were based on slavery. Even a relatively poor family owned at least one slave. Slaves who worked the farms in the countryside were housed away from their owners. Other slaves, who were educated, worked within the homes of the wealthy and acted as secretaries and stewards. The general view was that free people regarded work as the province of slaves. Wealthy free people spent long hours in the bathhouses, while the poorer free lounged around in the market places.

Aversion to work was emphatically not the outlook of the Wisdom books of the Bible.

Go to the ant, O sluggard; consider her ways, and be wise.[15]

Jews valued work based on this biblical tradition and, as noted, Israel was not a slave-based society. Typical of people in general, Jesus and his disciples worked with their hands in various trades. Many of Jesus' parables described the labors of peasants and fishermen.

In his letters Paul makes many references to working. He directed thieves no longer to steal but to work so as to have resources to help those in need.[16] He rebuked those who were idle, urging them to work in order to "earn their own living."[17]

Paul wrote to the church in Thessalonica, "We were not idle when we were with you, nor did we eat anyone's bread without paying for it, but with toil and labor we worked night and day, that we might not be a burden on

---

15. Prov 6:6.
16. Eph 4:28.
17. 2 Thess 3:6–13.

you."[18] Paul worked as a tent maker, an arduous task since tents were made of leather. The leather had been cured in horses' urine, so that tent making, with its connected activities of shoe repair and cobbling, was unhygienic, wearying labor. Paul lists the hard labor of tent making among his catalogues of sufferings.[19] Paul was determined to set an example of working to support himself and his colleagues and not be dependent on anyone.

Paul's view of himself was as of a servant of Jesus who preached the gospel and who supported himself by manual labor. There is no surviving contemporary description of Paul, but an observer may well have described him as an itinerant tradesman who also preached religion!

Meals

Jews would not enter the home of gentiles because they were regarded as "unclean." This was because gentiles ate foods that were classified as unclean or that had been rendered unclean by contact with gentiles. When challenged for the disciples' failure to wash hands (for religious not hygienic reasons), Jesus responded that food does not defile a person because it passes through the body as waste. Rather, he said that defilement is the result of evil that comes from within, from the heart.[20] Jesus' words liberated his disciples (who were Jews) from the restriction of eating only with fellow-Jews since all foods were now "clean."

In one stroke Jesus removed one of the great barriers against social fellowship in the world at that time.

The Christian was free to eat anything with anyone, Jew or gentile, because all food is "clean" and no food can defile the person who eats. At the same time, however, the Christian was free to accommodate to the person who was scrupulous about food that he thought brought defilement.[21] But that was a matter of discretion. This unselfish discretion went back to Jesus' teaching about loving one's neighbor.

---

18. 2 Thess 3:7–8.
19. 2 Cor 6:5; 11:23, 27; 1 Thess 2:9; 2 Thess 3:8.
20. Mark 7:14–23.
21. Rom 14:1–23.

The Love of Neighbor

Jesus taught about the love of neighbor in the remarkable *Parable of the Good Samaritan*. The injured man's Jewish fellow religionists "passed by on the other side," unwilling to help. The one who came to his side was a despised, unclean Samaritan. He went to extraordinary lengths to assist the man, including risking his own life and handing over money for the man's care. His love of neighbor was comprehensive and extended to the full recovery of the injured man.

Paul applied the principle of the love of neighbor to a Christian's social relationships with unbelievers. If an unbeliever invites Christians to a meal, let them go. Believers are free to eat whatever is placed on the table, including idol-sacrificed food.[22] If, however, someone mentions that the food has been sacrificed in a temple, Christians will not eat. Why? They will be concerned not to convey the idea that idolatry is a right thing to be engaged in. In other words, a believer's sacrificial example of not eating was to seek the "good" of his neighbor, to show that idolatry is an evil to be turned from.

In other words, while the Christian is free to eat whatever is on the table (because idolatry is not based in reality since there are no gods), nevertheless, there is a higher calling, the divine call to seek the good of one's neighbor. The Christian will not insist on freedom but where necessary will act in self-sacrifice for the good of the neighbor, to teach that idolatry is false worship and contrary to the revealed will of God.

Paul, Inventor of the Individual

Secular historian Larry Siedentop asks the question: "Was Paul the greatest revolutionary in human history?"[23] The argument of Siedentop's book is "yes," Paul was that inventor. He observes:

> For Paul the love of God revealed in the Christ imposes opportunities and obligations on the individual as such, that is, on conscience.... In one sense, Paul's conception of the Christ introduces the individual, by giving conscience a universal dimension.[24]

---

22. 1 Cor 10:23—11:1.

23. Siedentop, *Inventing the Individual*, 353.

24. Siedentop, *Inventing the Individual*, 352. Curiously, Siedentop says relatively little about Jesus and nothing about Martin Luther.

As the great promoter of Christ, his values and ethics, Paul unleashed a moral and intellectual force that has become a given within liberal democracy. If Siedentop is correct, as many critics have found him to be, then we have yet another remarkable contribution of Paul's to add to his list of achievements.

Paul's Spiritual Influence

In the short term, Paul's legacy was establishing churches in an arc from Jerusalem to Illyricum[25] that would become the basis for the Christian empire of the east, based in Constantinople, an empire that lasted more than a millennium (AD 313–1453). In the longer term, Paul's legacy has been expressed through his letters that are part of the canon of the Bible. The dominant theme in those letters is to point to the uniquely transcendent figure of Jesus the Lord.

Serving Jesus the Lord

For Paul, Jesus was first and foremost "the Lord." Remarkably, this is the same word that the prophets in the Old Testament used to refer to the "LORD" God Almighty.

In the Greek Old Testament (called the Septuagint) the word used for LORD is *Kyrios*, which is the word Paul uses for the *Lord* Jesus. In the panel following we quote first Isa 45:22–24 where he refers to the unique majesty of the LORD God. Next to it are Paul's words about Jesus, which are given in terms similar to those as Isaiah's.

---

25. Rom 15:19.

Turn to me and be saved, all the ends of the earth! For I am God, and there is no other.	Therefore God has highly exalted him and bestowed on him the name that is above every name,
By myself I have sworn; from my mouth has gone out in righteousness a word that shall not return:	so that at the name of Jesus every *knee* should bow, in heaven and on earth and under the earth, and every *tongue* confess
To me every *knee* shall bow, every *tongue* shall swear allegiance.'	that Jesus Christ is *Lord*, to the glory of God the Father.
Only in the LORD, it shall be said of me, are righteousness and strength.	(Phil 2:9–11)
(Isa 45:22–24)	

Paul was identifying the resurrected and "highly exalted" Jesus with the LORD God of whom Isaiah wrote. This Jesus is the "Lord" before whom "every knee is to bow" and whom "every tongue" will "confess."

In his letters Paul uses the word *Kyrios,* referring to Jesus, 385 times, for example:

> If you confess with your mouth that Jesus is *Lord* and believe in your heart that God raised him from the dead, you will be saved.[26]
>
> I want you to understand that no one . . . can say "Jesus is *Lord*" except in the Holy Spirit."[27]
>
> For what we proclaim is not ourselves, but Jesus Christ as Lord, with ourselves as your servants for Jesus.[28]

From the blazing glory outside Damascus Jesus *the Lord* confronted Paul the persecutor. From that time, both in preaching and in letter writing, Paul repeatedly declared that "Jesus is Lord."

The Lordship of Jesus was implicit within the earthly ministry of Jesus but that became explicit after his resurrection and ascension. Among the apostles no one declared that truth more vigorously or persistently than the former Pharisee, Paul. That is a significant part of the legacy of Paul.

---

26. Rom 10:9.

27. 1 Cor 12:3.

28. 2 Cor 4:5.

The Legacy of Paul

The Revealing of the Son of God

Closely related is Paul's repeated reference to Jesus as *the Son of God*. This, too, flowed from what happened outside Damascus. Paul testified that "God... was pleased to reveal *his Son* to me, in order that I might preach him among the gentiles."[29]

The Acts of the Apostles confirms this, so that in Damascus "immediately Paul proclaimed Jesus in the synagogues, saying, 'He is the Son of God.'"[30]

Paul refers to Jesus as the Son of God no less than forty times in his letters. His teaching that Jesus was the Son of God was a foundational belief in the churches Paul established.

Strikingly, Paul connects Jesus the Son of God *intimately* and *uniquely* with God, his Father.

"God sent his *own* Son..."	Rom 8:3
"God did not spare his *own* Son..."	Rom 8:32

Paul's teaching about the Son's exclusive and personal relationship with his Father is consistent with Jesus' own words: "No one knows *the* Son except *the* Father, and no one knows *the* Father except *the* Son."[31]

Through Paul's teaching we understand the inner relationship within the being of God: "Blessed be the God and Father of our Lord Jesus Christ."[32] God is the Father of his own Son, who is our Lord, Jesus Christ.

God's revelation to Paul the Pharisee about the hitherto unknown inner relationship of the Son of God with his Father enabled generations of subsequent Christians to relate to God in deeply personal ways. Through their trust in the Son, God has adopted them into his extended family of adopted sons and daughters of the Father.

The Cross of Christ and the Righteousness of God

Once again Paul's Damascus Road experience proved formative and affected his thinking as reflected in his letters from first to last over an almost two decade long period (AD 48–65).

---

29. Gal 1:16.
30. Acts 9:20.
31. Matt 11:25.
32. 2 Cor 1:3.

Paul the Pharisee had been an attempted but failed keeper of the law of God who became a persecutor of the followers of Jesus, whom he regarded as a false messiah, who had been "hanged on a tree." When the heavenly Jesus addressed Paul from the glory of God he came to realize two things simultaneously. One was that Jesus had suffered the curse of God for him, for his forgiveness as a persecutor. The other was that in his death Jesus had fulfilled the absolute requirements of the law of God that no one, Paul included, was capable of keeping.

When Paul preached to gentiles he called on them to commit to Christ apart from the necessary engagement with Jewish practices like male circumcision, dietary rules, purity practices, or the observation of the feasts of the Jewish religious calendar. Paul referred to these as "works of the law," which carried the double meaning of the "out*workings* of the law" and the "*works* to fulfill the demands of the law," that is, based on human *work*. For Paul, the death of Jesus had completely fulfilled the just requirements of the law of God so that such attempted "works of the law" negated and detracted from the unique achievements of Jesus' death.

Some of Paul's fellow-Jewish Christians passionately believed that to be acceptable to God and to them as God's covenant people the gentile believers *must* submit to "works of the law," in particular, to male circumcision. For a period even Peter went along with this teaching (in relation to dietary rules). Paul had to inform him that even Jews like them were not justified by "works of the law" but only "by faith" in Jesus Christ:

> We ourselves are Jews by birth and not gentile sinners; yet we know that a person is not justified by works of the law but through faith in Jesus Christ, so we also have believed in Christ Jesus, in order to be justified by faith in Christ and not by works of the law, because by works of the law no one will be justified.[33]

Since Galatians is Paul's first letter, it means it is Paul's first reference to his keyword "justified."

"Justified" is a legal word meaning "God's single act of declaring a person acquitted, accepted by God." God does that on the basis of a person's "faith" commitment to Jesus, not by "works of the law."

---

33. Gal 2:15–6.

The Legacy of Paul

Paul and the Reformation

In the sixteenth century Father Martin Luther, a professor of biblical studies in Wittenberg, Germany, applied Paul's teaching to aberrations in current Catholic thinking. The teaching of the church was that Christians received merit from God based on religious acts like the veneration of relics, the lighting of candles, pilgrimages, and the payment of money for indulgences that cancelled one's sins and the sins of those in purgatory.

Although the precise situations were different Luther, based on his study of Romans and Galatians, came to believe that the same issues of merit based on "works of the law" applied, as in Paul's day.

Paul's campaign against Jewish Christian advocacy of "works of the law" inspired Luther to fight for "justification by faith alone." This doctrine became the signature belief of the new Reformation movement that quickly spread throughout Europe. It is, perhaps, the greatest legacy of Paul, one that came into its own fifteen hundred years after his death.

For Paul to be "justified by faith" was inseparable from doctrine of the vicarious death of the Son of God. This explains why in his preaching and in his letters to the churches he constantly referred to the cross of Christ. As law-breakers the plight of humans is dire. Only Christ's saving death meets man at the point of his deepest need. No truth was more deeply held by Paul than this, nor by Martin Luther all those years later.

The Reformation, although based on Paul's teaching on justification by faith alone, was not a narrowly religious movement. From its beginnings in Wittenberg in 1517 it quickly became also a political movement, one that contributed to the destruction of the Hapsburg Empire and the emergence of independent countries like Germany. In effect, Paul's teachings, as promoted by Luther, changed the course of history fifteen hundred years later.

It is no exaggeration to say that Paul's proclamation of Jesus the Lord as the only Savior of sinners continues to have profound influence. This sublime truth continues to save individuals outside the churches but equally proves to be the great spiritual reality that brings revival to churches and denominations that have lost their way and slipped into empty social and political programs.

Conclusion

It is fair to claim that the influence of Paul through his letters have made him the person of most enduring influence from the epoch of Greek and Roman antiquity. The writings of Plato, Cicero, and Seneca continue to be of interest in modern times but these are of lesser importance compared to the epistles of Paul, the servant of Jesus.

Paul's major influence is primarily his teaching about Jesus the Lord, who is the Son of God, whose death is the source of divine acceptance of lost humanity. This authoritative teaching about Jesus issues in considerable subsidiary interest in his ethical teachings, for example, about God and Caesar, slavery, the importance of work, the end of eating taboos, love of neighbor, and gender and family relationships.

When Paul's ethical directions are examined in relation to Jesus' instructions we may say that Paul made effective and valiant efforts to apply his Lord's teaching to a world very different from that of Galilee and Judea, the world of the Greeks and the Romans.

One thing to emphasize is that Paul did not set out to make a name for himself. We recall his words, "We preach not ourselves but Jesus Christ as Lord, and ourselves your servants for Jesus' sake."[34] Paul's sole purpose was to make Jesus' name great, which he did to a remarkable degree. While humbly engaged in doing that, however, he secured a unique place for himself in the annals of history.

---

34. 2 Cor 4:5 (my translation).

Bibliography

Barker, Ernest. *From Alexander to Constantine: Passages and Documents Illustrating the History of Social and Political Ideas, 336 BC–AD 337*. Oxford: Oxford University Press, 1954.

Barrett, C. K. *A Commentary on the Second Epistle to the Corinthians*. London: A & C Black, 1973.

Bird, Michael. "Reassessing a Rhetorical Approach to Paul's Letters." *Expository Times* 119/8 (2008) 374–79.

Bockmuehl, Marcus. *Simon Peter in Scripture and Memory*. Grand Rapids: Baker Academic, 2012.

Bruce, F. F. *The Acts of the Apostles: Greek Text with Introduction and Commentary*. Grand Rapids: Eerdmans, 1990.

———. *Paul: Apostle of the Free Spirit*. Exeter: Paternoster, 1977.

———. "The Spirit in the Letter to the Galatians." In *Essays on Apostolic Themes*, edited by P. Elbert, 36–48. Peabody, MA: Hendrickson, 1985.

Doyle, A. D. "Pilate's Career and the Date of the Crucifixion." *Journal of Theological Studies* 42 (1941) 190–93.

Dunn, James D. G. *The Theology of Paul the Apostle*. Grand Rapids: Eerdmans, 1998.

Fitzmyer, Joseph. *Luke the Theologian: Aspects of His Teaching*. London: Geoffrey Chapman, 1989.

Flew, Anthony. *There Is a God: How the World's Most Notorious Atheist Changed His Mind*. San Francisco: HarperOne, 2007.

Gagnon, Robert. *The Bible and Homosexual Practice*. Nashville: Abingdon, 2001.

Gray, Patrick. *Paul as a Problem in History and Culture*. Grand Rapids: Baker Academic, 2016.

Hengel, Martin. *Acts and the History of Earliest Christianity*. London: SCM, 1979 ET.

———. *Between Jesus and Paul: Studies in the Earliest History of Christianity*. London: SCM, 1983 ET.

———. *The Pre-Christian Paul*. London: SCM, 1991 ET.

Hengel, Martin, and Anna Maria Schwemer. *Between Damascus and Antioch: The Unknown Years*. Louisville: Westminster John Knox, 1997 ET.

Jeremias, Joachim. *Jerusalem in the Time of Jesus*. London: SCM, 1969 ET.

Jerome, Saint. *On Illustrious Men*. Fathers of the Church 100. Washington, DC: Catholic University of America Press, 1999.

Bibliography

Lefkowitz, Mary R., and Maureen B. Fant, eds. *Women's Life in Greece and Rome*. Baltimore: Johns Hopkins Press, 1982.

Maier, P. L. "The Episode of the Golden Roman Shields at Jerusalem." *Harvard Theological Review* 62 (1969) 109–21.

———. "Sejanus, Pilate and the Date of the Crucifixion." *Church History* 37 (1968) 3–13.

Murphy-O'Connor, Jerome. *Paul: A Critical Life*. Oxford: Oxford University Press, 1997.

Porter, Stanley. "Paul and the Pauline Letter Collection." In *Paul and the Second Century*, edited by Michael Bird and Joseph Dodson, 19–36. London: T. & T. Clark, 2011.

Richards, E. Randolph. *Paul and First Century Letter-Writing*. Downers Grove, IL: InterVarsity, 2004.

Sherwin-White, A. N. *The Roman Citizenship*. 2nd ed. Oxford: Clarendon, 1973.

Siedentop, Larry. *Inventing the Individual: The Origins of Western Liberalism*. London: Penguin, 2015.

Smallwood, E. Mary. "Some Notes on the Jews Under Tiberius." *Latomus* 15 (1956) 314–29.

Thornton, B. S. *Eros*. Boulder, CO: Westview, 1997.

Unnik, W. C. van. "Tarsus or Jerusalem: The City of Paul's Youth?" In *Sparsa Collecta, Part 1: Evangelia, Paulina, Acta*, by W. C. Van Unnik, 259–320. Novum Testamentum 29. Leiden: Brill, 1973.

Wilson, Emily. *Seneca: A Life*. London: Random House, 2014.

Wrede, William. *Paul*. Boston: American Unitarian Association, 1908 ET.

Wright, Tom. *Paul: A Biography*. London: SPCK, 2018.

Name and Subject Index

Abraham, 7, 15, 29, 54–55, 66, 67, 68, 112, 156
Achaia, 24, 40, 42, 44, 45, 46, 60, 71, 80, 81, 87, 94, 97
Aegean provinces, 40, 43–44, 80, 85, 87, 90, 92, 94, 95, 100, 109, 87
Alexander the Coppersmith, 87
Alexander the Great, 68, 112
Alexandria Troas, 13, 42, 43, 44, 47, 86, 93, 95, 96, 102
Antioch in Syria, 16, 22, 33, 34, 37, 38, 39, 41, 61, 65, 68, 79, 80, 85, 88, 95, 96, 101, 104, 126, 127, 132, 154, 156
Antioch crisis, 39–39, 68
Antioch in Pisidia, 17, 38, 52, 112, 133, 134
Athens, 2, 16, 41, 97
Apollos, 86, 99, 100, 130
Appian Way, 40, 93, 105
Arabia, 1, 2, 31, 32, 33, 49, 57, 78, 126
Asia, 42, 44, 45, 47, 60, 71, 80, 81, 86, 87, 89, 93, 94
Augustus Caesar, 132–33
Barnabas, 37, 38, 39, 65, 68, 79, 85, 87, 88, 94, 101
Archippus, 84, 85, 100
Aristarchus, 84, 85, 100
Barrett, C. K., 35n15
Berea, 12, 40, 44, 80, 102
Bruce, F.F., x
Burrus, Sextus Afranius, 46, 47
Byzantine Empire, 82
Claudius, 40, 41, 45, 94, 98, 107, 48

Clement of Rome, 11
Christian origins, 108
Collection, the 42, 43, 92, 101, 103, 104
collections of Paul's Letters, 10–12
Concord (*homonoia*), 68
Corinth, x, 5, 6, 12, 17, 20, 39, 40, 41, 42–43, 44, 46, 48, 51, 61, 63, 72, 74, 76, 80, 88, 90, 91, 92, 97, 98, 99, 100, 101, 102, 103, 104, 105, 106, 111, 114, 127, 128, 129, 130, 133, 134, 162
Colossae, 44, 80, 84, 100
Crete, 103–5
Critics of Paul, 6, 7
Damascus, 2, 3, 8, 9, 10, 19, 27–30, 31–32, 33, 50, 52, 57, 58, 65, 71, 78, 79, 83, 87, 126, 131, 136, 148, 149, 152, 153, 158, 168, 169
dating Paul, 9–10
Demas, 84, 85, 87, 100
list of coworkers, 85–86
Dunn, James, 1, 154, 173
Dyrrachium, 40, 93
Easter "tradition," 69
Ebionites, 6
Egnatian Way, 40, 44, 93
envoys bearing letters, 105n51
Ephesus, 4, 12, 41–42, 43, 44, 47, 61, 72, 80, 82, 84, 86, 90, 92, 93, 94, 99, 100, 101, 104, 122
Epaphras, 84, 85, 100

Name and Subject Index

Epaphroditus, 86, 105,106–108, 109, 137
expulsion of Jews from Rome, 98
Fitzmyer, Joseph, 13
Galatia, 24, 37, 39, 41, 42, 45, 60, 71, 79, 81, 86, 87, 89, 126, 127
Gallio, 40, 45, 46
Gamaliel, 3, 4, 15, 19, 20–21, 24–25, 70, 83
"hardening" of Israel, the, 67
"Hebrews," 27
"Hellenists," 26–28
Hengel, Martin, 2, 13, 21, 33, , 95, 173
Herod Antipas, 32
Historical Jesus, 58
Homonoia, 68, 112
Irenaeus, 13, 95
Isaiah's "servant" poems, 52
James, brother of the Lord, 6, 30, 32, 33, 37, 39, 42, 58, 78, 88, 101, 145, 147, 148, 151
Jerusalem
    Antioch delegates visit (in AD 47), 101
    Conference (in AD 49), 78, 79
    conservative members, 126, 127, 132
    destination for the Collection, 97
    envoys from Jerusalem, 89
    Paul as student in, 83
    Paul returns to in AD 52, 101
    Paul stays with Peter, 71, 108, 145, 148
    Paul's final journey to in AD 57, 92
    Silvanus from, 88
Jesus as template for Christian behavior, 58
Jesus movement open to non-Jews, 1
John the Baptist, 9, 26, 99
King Aretas, 32
King Herod Agrippa II, 20
knowing about Paul, 10
Last Supper "tradition," 71
Lessing, G.E., 7
Luke,
    Aegean mission, 85
    From Antioch, 96
    anonymous author of Luke-Acts, 95
    beloved physician and scholar, 95–97
    in Ephesus, 100
    historian, 109
    Paul's "unknown" years, 36, 79
    Paul's westward missions, 35
    Peter's sermons, 57
    in Philippi, 96, 97
    reliability, 12–14
    "Saul who is also Paul," 38
    scholar, 95
    sources underlying Gospel of Luke, 64
    Syria and Cilicia, 33
    "we" passages, 12–14, 45, 80
    with Paul at the end, 93
Lydia, 99, 105, 106, 142
Mark, 38, 84, 85, 87, 94, 100
Macedonia, 1, 42, 43, 44, 45, 46, 47, 60, 68, 71, 80, 81, 86, 87, 90, 91, 92, 93, 97, 102, 112, 122
Muratorian Canon, 11, 13
Murphy-O'Connor, Jerome, x, 17
Nabataea, 51
New Perspective on Paul, 153–158
Nietzche, Friedrich, 7
Oxyrhynchus, 10
P^{45}, 10–12
Paul
    as persecutor, 18, 26–27
    as strategist, 4
    Christian mind, the, 120–25
    coworkers, 83–109
    cross of Christ and the righteousness of God, 169–70
    death, 48
    defense of, 8
    devotion to Jesus, 2, 3
    early life, 14–15
    elitism, 129–131
    example of Jesus, the, 5, 57–60
    education, 17
    ethical influence, 158–61
    fellow-workers, 5

Name and Subject Index

founder of Christianity?, 144–45
Gamaliel, under, 24–25
Gentile churches, 34–35
gospel to fellow-Jews, 52
Greek Bible, 4
hardships, 2, 3
historical Jesus, the, 146–49
homosexuality, 137–40
house tables, 74
"in Christ," 29
in Jerusalem, 20–21, 25–26, 37
in Palestine 44–45
influence on the Reformation, 171
intellect, 3
invention of the individual, 166–67
kinsmen, 18
legalism, 126–27
letter to the Philippians, 45–46
letter-writer, as, 3, 83, 83
letters as Scripture, 150–51
libertinism, 128–29
light to the nations, 52
married?, 21
membership, 108–15
message: God's Son, 50
missions in Cyprus, Pisidia, Lycaonia, 37–39
mission network, 78–
name, 20
old covenant ended, 53–54
olive tree, 56
on death, 117
on love of neighbor, 165
on man-woman relationships, 141–43
on marriage, 162–64
on meals, 165
on the return of Jesus, 149–50
on triumphalism, 131–32
on work, 163–65
on wisdom of God, 118
Pharisee, a, 21, 29
"preaching the faith", 33
priority: to the Jews first, 66
promise to Abraham, the, 29

Qur'an, and the, 7
Roman Citizen, 3, 4, 9, 17, 18, 20, 25, 45, 48, 131, 132, 133, 153, 159
release from prison in Rome, 47
Septuagint, use of, 25
slavery, 161–62
socially superior to Jesus, 3
spiritual world, 115–16
Stephen, 25
synagogue beatings, 35
Tarsus, 16, 17, 18
team problems, 87
"thorn," the, 36
Titus, 85, 86, 87, 100, 101, 102–5, 109
"Traditions," 70–77
tribe of Benjamin, 17
unique achievements, 2
"unknown years," 36
words of Jesus, deference to, 60–64
"zeal," 18–20

Peter, 8, 11, 30, 32–33, 39, 48, 54, 55, 57, 58, 62, 65, 68, 71, 78, 88, 89, 143, 145, 147, 148, 149, 151, 152, 156, 170
Phasaelis, daughter of Aretas, 32
Pharisees, 19, 21, 22–24, 26, 127, 131, 134
Philippi, 3, 13, 17, 37, 40, 44, 46, 80, 81, 86, 92, 95, 96, 97, 99, 105, 106, 107, 108, 122, 123, 127, 129, 130, 137
Philemon, 84, 85, 90, 100, 109, 137
Phoebe, 85, 99, 105–6, 109, 142
Pontius Pilate, 25, 26, 147
Priscilla and Aquila, 85, 97–100, 105, 109, 142
Qumran community, 21
Reformers' attack on religious "works," 49
Remembrance Meal, 68, 111
Rome, 88, 89, 90, 92, 93, 94, 96, 97, 98, 99, 101, 105, 106, 107, 112, 129, 130, 132, 137, 150, 164

Name and Subject Index

Sejanus L. Aelius, Praetorian Prefect, 25
Seneca, Lucius Annaeus, 46, 47, 172
Silvanus, 51, 85, 88–89, 90, 94, 95, 96, 105, 109
Stephen, 19, 23, 25, 26–27, 28
Sources of the Synoptic Gospels, 60–64
Renan, Ernst, 7
Schweitzer, Albert, 7
Tacitus Publius Cornelius, 1, 9, 25, 48, 115
Thessalonica, 40, 44, 51, 61, 73, 80, 16
Tiberius Caesar, 9, 25, 73, 160
Tigellinus Gaius Ofonius, Praetorian Prefect, 47
Timothy, 11, 12, 43, 51, 80, 81, 87, 89, 90, 91, 92, 93, 94, 95, 96, 100, 101, 102, 104, 105, 109, 137
Tychicus, 84, 105,
Wright, Tom, x

Scripture Index

OLD TESTAMENT

Genesis
1:31	123n9
15:6	157n14
2:24	143n19
12:3	29n67

Exodus
21:2	161n3
34:29–35	29n64

Leviticus
18:1–3	141n13
18:22	139n7
20:13	139n8
29:13	141n13

Deuteronomy
6:4	55n31
21:23	28n60, 56n22

Joshua
8:27–27	28n61

Proverbs
6:6	164n15

Isaiah
45:22–24	168
49:6	52n12

Jeremiah
31:31–34	155n7

NEW TESTAMENT

Matthew
10:10	62
11:25	169n31
11:27	51n5
11:28–29	127n3

Mark
2:15	22n26
2:18	22n27
2:23–26	22n28
7:1	22n29
7:14–23	165n20
10:6–9	163n12
10:11	61n11
12:17	160n2
13:32	51n5
15:7	26n52

Scripture Index

Luke

3:1–2	9n1
5:30	23n34
6:11, 13–14	23n40
6:14	23n38
6:15	19n14
7:34	23n35
10:7	62
10:29	23n39
11:39, 42	23n36
11:43	23n37
12:1	23n36
13:1	26n52
14:7, 12–14	23n37
15:1–2	23n35
18:11	131n14
22:20	156n8
22:19–20	63n14

John

8:31–32	161n4
9:13–16	23n33
9:22	23n33

Acts

1:13	19n14
3:1	26n55
5:34	24n43
6:9	2549
6:9–14	25n48
7:58	9n2
8:3	27n56
9:1–3	9n3, 28n60
9:4	28n62
9:7	30n72
9:16	3n7
9:18	30n69
9:19–22	31
9:20	169n30
9:21	20n15
9:23–30	33n7
9:25	87n3
9:30	33n7
9:31	16n1
9:32—11:18	33n9
11:25–30	33n6
12:25	33n6
13:1	96n31
13:36–47	52n13
13:47	53n14
15:1	127n1
15:5	24n42
15:22–23	34n12
15:23, 41	51n9, 79n6
15:32; 16:37	88n11
15:41	34n13
16:1, 4–5	79n8
16:2	89n13
16:5–6	96n33
16:10–12	96n13
16:23; 17:9, 14; 18:12	41n27
18:1–2	40n23
18:12–16	46
18:23	79n8
19:10	44n30
20:3	103n45
20:5—21:18	13n11
21:39	16n1
22:3	20n18, 25n46
22:3–5	19n12
22:9	30n72
22:28	17n3
23:16	21n21
26:4	20n19
26:10–11	27n57
27:1—28:16	13n11
28:16	45n33, 47n40

Romans

1:9	51n6
1:1, 5	30n74
1:13	76n21
1:14, 16	153n1
1:20	117n7
1:18–23	117n6
1:26–27	138n5
3:9	116n3
3:23	117n4
3:26	123n6
3:28–30	153n2
5:12	117n9
6:9	74n14

Scripture Index

6:17	70n1, 75n17	2:16	144n22
7:2	163n11	4:4	135n2, 13n3
8:3, 32	51n4	4:9	133n18
9:7–9	56n23	4:15–16	113n10
10:4	53n15	4:16	5n14
10:9	168n26	4:17	90n15
10:21	53n16	5:1	101n38
11:1	15	6:9–11	138n6, 163n8
11:13–24	56	6:12	128n4
11:25	76n21	7:2, 39	163n11
11:25–32	37n18	7:3	142n18
12:2	116n1	7:7, 9, 38, 40	21n22
12:7	106n53	7:10	142n21
12:14	63	7:10–11	61n10
12:17	63	7:17	81n10
12:18	64	7:19	128n6
12:20	64	7:21	161n6
13:1–7	160n1	8:6	148n3
13:7	64, 160n2	9:4	21n21
13:9	129n7	9:6	87n6
14:1–23	165n21	9:14	62n12
14:1—15:7	154n6	9:17	30n74
14:14	64	10:23	128n5
14:20	64	10:23—11:1	166n22
15:1–3	59n6	10:33—11:1	60n8, 114n15
15:5–7	114n14	10:33	5n13
15:7	5n13	11:1	5n14, 113n11
15:7–9	59n7	11:2	70n1, 74n15, 141n15
15:8–9	66n1		
15:12	150n9	11:2–16	162n8
15:19	167n25	11:5, 10	74n11
15:20–21	45n32	11:11	142n17
16:1–2	105n50	11:16	75n19, 81n10
16:3–5	98	11:21–22	130n13
16:4, 16	81n10	11:23	74n15
16:8–10	91n17	11:23–25	33n5, 62n13, 71n4, 77
16:17	70n1, 75n18		
16:21	90n16	11:25	156n8
16:23	5n12, 103n45	12:1	76n20, 21
		12:3	168n27
1 Corinthians		12:7	111n2, 130n9
		12:25	130n10
1:11	130n10	14:12	110n1, 121n3
1:21	118n11	14:19	121n1
1:26	111n4	14:23	5n12, 114n16
1:31	132n17	14:26	121n2
2:6	118n10	14:37	151n13

Scripture Index

1 Corinthians (*continued*)

15:1–3	74n15
15:1–7	77
15:3–7	33n5, 71n2
15:7–11; 15:9–21	39n22
15:11	58n2
15:12–58	76
15:20, 23	150n8
15:26	117n8
15:30, 32; 16:9	41n27
15:33	18n8
15:51	149n6

2 Corinthians

1:1	44n29
1:3	169n32
1:5	3n9
1:9	41n27
1:19	51n7
2:1	101n39
2:4	102n40
2:3–4; 2:13	43n28
2:14–16	134n19
2:17	102n43
3:6	156n9
4:1	29n65
4:2	122n4
4:4	117n5
4:5	50n3, 168n28, 172n34
4:6	30n73
5:1	74n13
5:1–11	102n41
5:14	3n6
5:15	29n68
5:17	29n66, 30n73, 30n75
6:5	165n19
6:8	123n8
8:6	101n37
8:18–19	97n34
8:9	5n13, 59n3, 113n12, 149n5
10:1	5n13, 59n5
10:8	151n14
11:1—12:13	76

11:2	20n16, 123n12
11:4–5	102n42
11:22–23	15
11:22—12:13	84n2, 134n20
11:23, 27	165n19
11:24	27n59, 35n14, 79n5
11:23–25	3n8
11:28	44n31
11:31	32n4
12:2, 7	36n17
12:16–18	102n44
13:10	151n14

Galatians

1:2	79n7
1:4	116n2
1:6	30n73
1:13, 21	26n54
1:13–14	15, 19n11
1:14	24n45
1:15–16	50
1:16	3n5, 28n63, 78n1, 169n29
1:17	31n2, 32n3
1:18	71n2
1:18–19	30n70, 58n1, 145n24, 148n1
1:21–24	34n10, 79n4
1:23	51n8, 84n1
2:1–9	101n36, 145n25
2:2	58n2
2:3, 14; 5:12	39n21
2:5, 14	39n20
2:7–8	7bn3
2:8	78n2
2:1–9	37
2:11–13	156n10
2:11–14	127n1, 154n5
2:11–16	156n11
2:15–16	54, 170n33
2:16	74n12
2:20	3n4
3:1	26n53
3:6–9	55n19
3:6–14	54
3:10–11	157n16

3:10–14	55n20	3:7–8	131n16
3:17	157n13	3:10	2n3
3:25	157n15	3:12	30n71, 30n75
3:26–29	68n4	3:17	5n14
3:27–28	154n4	4:22	47n40
3:28	112		
3:28–29	112n6	**Colossians**	
4:4	148n2	2:8	70n1
4:21	156n12	3:11	112n8
5:1	126n2, 161n5	3:18—21	163n14
6:2	111n5	3:18—4:1	74n10
		4:14	13n14
Ephesians		4:17	151n12
1:18	113n9		
2:11–13	67n2	**1 Thessalonians**	
2:14–17	67n3	1:8–10	72n5, 149n7
2:19	112n7	2:9	165n19
4:20–21	74n16	2:9–10	51n10
4:28	129n8, 164n16	4:1–2	72n6
5:1	60n9	4:1–12	77
5:22–33	142n16	4:3–8	163n11
5:22—6:9	74n10, 163n14	4:13	76n21
5:33	74n11	4:15	149n6
6:9	161n6	5:7	73n8
		5:9–10	52n11
Philippians			
1:7	46n3	**2 Thessalonians**	
1:13	45n35, 47n40	1:4	81n10
1:25–26	46n37	2:3	150n11
1:27	130n11	2:14; 3:6	70n1
1:29	3n10	3:6–13	164n17
2:3,14	130n11	3:7, 9	5n14
2:4–7	114n13	3:7–8	165n18
2:5	5n13	3:8	165n19
2:5–8	59n4	3:15	74n16
2:5–11	148n4		
2:9–11	168	**1 Timothy**	
2:19	92n20	1:2	90n15
2:20	90n15, 95n30	1:3	92n21
2:24	92n19	1:3–7	93n22
2:25	107n56	1:3; 3:14	47
2:25–30	106n54	1:8–11	139
3:5	21n24	1:15	5n15
3:6	23n41	4:14	89n14
3:5–6	15, 17n7		
3:5–7	131n15		

2 Timothy

1:2	90n15
1:6	89n14
1:8	93n23, 93n23
1:15	87n8, 73n24, 93n24
2:2	87n4
2:1–2	94n29
3:1	87n5, 93n25
4:10, 14	87n9, 104n49
4:11	13n14, 93n27
4:13	93n28
4:13, 30	47

Titus

1:5	47, 103n47
2:1, 7–8	103n48
2:2	122n5
3:12	47, 103n46

Philemon

2	107n55
7	162n7
10	136n4
21	162n8

Hebrews

12:23	92n18

1 Peter

3:1	143n20
5:12	88n10, 89n12

2 Peter

3:15–17	151n15
3:16	11n8

OTHER ANCIENT TEXTS

Intertestamental texts

Wisdom

6:17–18	157n17

Sirach

3:3–4, 14	157n18

1 Maccabees

2:27	19n10

First Century Jewish texts

Josephus

Jewish War

1.648–53	19n13
2.162	21n25
2.169–77	26n52

Jewish Antiquities

18.55–62	26n52

Against Apion

2.190–219	74n10
2:199–202	140n10

Philo

Special Laws

2.253	22n31

Flaccus

1:1	25n50

Embassy to Gaius

159–160	25n50
299, 302	26n52

Scripture Index

Apology for the Jews
7:14

Later Jewish Texts

Mishnah

Aboth
5:21   9n4, 21n23
6:7   157n19

Sotah
9:15   24n44

Makkot
3:16   158n20

Talmud
bSanhedrin 97.a   22n30

Roman texts

Suetonius

Julius Caesar
1.52.3   141

Tiberius
48, 65   25n50

Claudius
25.4   40n23, 25

Tacitus

Annals
3.72   25n50
4.2, 272   25n50
15.44   9n5

Patristic texts

1 Clement
5:1–5   48n1

Ancient Greek

Aristotle

Nichomachean Ethics
1162a

www.ingramcontent.com/pod-product-compliance
Lightning Source LLC
Chambersburg PA
CBHW031432150426
43191CB00006B/487